Black Gospel /
White Church

BLACK GOSPEL / WHITE CHURCH

JOHN M. BURGESS

THE SEABURY PRESS   NEW YORK

1982
The Seabury Press
815 Second Avenue
New York, N.Y. 10017

Library of Congress Cataloging in Publication Data
Main entry under title:

Black gospel/white church.

1. Afro-Americans—Religion—Addresses, essays, lectures. 2. Episcopal Church—
Sermons. 3. Sermons, American. I. Burgess, John M.
BR563.N4B57   252'.0373'08996073   81-18197
ISBN 0-8164-0511-5

AACR2

To Kenneth Hughes,
who preached the Word
not only with his lips
but with his life

Acknowledgments

I wish to acknowledge my gratitude to those who have made this book possible through the contribution of their own sermons, and to the relatives and friends of authors now deceased. I am especially indebted to the resources of the following libraries: the library of the General Theological Seminary, New York; the Sterling Memorial Library and the Beinecke Rare Book and Manuscript Library of Yale University, New Haven, CT; and the New York Public Library, Schomburg Center for Research in Black Culture.

I am also grateful for the help of the following friends who have contributed very pertinent suggestions: the Reverend Professor Nathan Wright, Jr., University of New York at Albany and Professor Otey M. Scruggs, Syracuse University.

Contents

Introduction

There are those who will object to the title of this book. The Christian Gospel is color-blind—neither Jewish nor gentile, neither male nor female, neither bond nor free. This is especially emphasized by those who have been special beneficiaries of a Christian establishment based on the assumption that the Gospel is, of course, white—and American. The miracle of the Gospel of Christ is that, although it is one in its message, it has the quality of being readily expressed in every culture, ethnic group, or race—if Christians will allow it! Too much of the history of Christian missions has been the dreary tale of the propagating of the Western way of life in the name of Christ. That this bias is now changing is largely due to new, nonwhite Christians who, having received the Gospel, are making it their own in terms that have meaning within their own cultures. That Christianity is making spectacular strides in Africa today is the result of the actual withdrawal of Western missionaries from positions of authority and of the preaching of the Word by blacks to blacks.

American Christians must realize that this same process has been going on among their black brothers and sisters since the days when they as African slaves were brought within the Christian fold. Whites have tried in every way possible to convince blacks that God is white. As Christians, blacks have been expected to demonstrate a patience, a love, and a tolerence they rarely saw in their teachers and oppressors; but they have, nevertheless, made this Gospel their own. Steeped in the despondency of powerlessness, cursed by the ever-present insufficiency of the means of livelihood, relegated to racist institutions, condemned by injustice, and propagandized by notions of white supremacy and black degeneracy, blacks have taken the Gospel given to them by those who would use it as an instrument of their pacification and have transformed it into a means of liberation.

The black minorities in largely white churches have been especially subject to this attempt to make them into something other than what they are. It is the common impression among many blacks as well as whites that this strategy has succeeded, and that blacks in white churches have alienated themselves from the concerns of the black community. The large black denominations have charged that these folk have turned their backs on the black religious heritage, and have chosen to identify with the white community to facilitate their opportunistic climb up the American ladder of success.

The early founders of black churches were not so sure. When Richard Allen and Absalom Jones set up their black congregations in Philadelphia at the end of the eighteenth century, there was no great dispute between these close friends about the different roads they chose to take. Allen founded the Bethel African Methodist Episcopal Church with the intention of creating a separate black denomination. Jones founded the African Episcopal Church of St. Thomas as a congregation *within* the Episcopal diocese of Pennsylvania. Both men continued to be outstanding leaders in their community, and shared their ministries in every possible way. Episcopalian Jones and Methodist Allen minimized differences in polity and theology in their common understanding that the important ministry of each was the preaching of the Gospel by blacks to blacks. Although Allen was a most ardent advocate of the Methodist position, he at no time took the attitude that his people were "naturally" so. His mature and catholic wisdom make mockery of many of his successors who have been convinced that blacks in white denominations have nothing to say that can give hope and freedom to their people.

The sermons and addresses included in this book are presented as evidence of the black Episcopal clergy's continuing concern for their community. They have, in fact, been loyal to both church and community. Seventy-five years ago, Dr. W. E. B. Du Bois described the "two-ness" of the American black, and his analysis is cited by the Reverend Nathan Baxter in this volume. Blacks who try to maintain some sense of equilibrium between black tradition and white institutionalism have no easy time of it. Yet, we see in these sermons an honest effort to deal with this situation on the part of several contributors who almost blatantly stress their racial loyalty while at the same time insisting that their congregations be aware of the moral imperatives of the society of which they are a part. In this process, they save themselves from that form of demagoguery that revels in describing the racism of whites and refuses to come to terms with the moral demands required of blacks. Our clergy have had to work as evangelists beset on one side by black Christians who doubt the integrity of their message, and on the other by white Christians who undermine their own message by their racism. These black evangelists encouraged their own people to resist, to fight for change, to aspire, and to hope. Because they were validly ordained priests, they were able to carry their challenge into the conventions and councils of the larger church, and they spoke not as guests or outside petitioners, but as a part of the church itself. They are a significant portion of the history of the Episcopal Church and a portion that has been ignored, minimized, and even ridiculed; yet the Episcopal Church is what it is today because of this historic symbiosis of black and white within its fellowship.

The Episcopal Church does not stand alone in this studied avoidance of the contribution that blacks have made to American society. Until recently, scholars have successfully withheld mention of blacks in history except when it served purposes that had meaning for whites. The advent of "black awareness" has revealed the ever-present undercurrent of the experience of black people who "lived, worked, fought, and died" as citizens of the United States, and no history is complete that continues to ignore them. To add the black experience to the story can often change the evaluation of personalities and events. For example, William White, the first bishop of Pennsylvania and chief organizer of the church after the Revolution, is still regarded as "the foremost ecclesiastical statesman of his times." Black church-people can insert into the record, however, that Bishop White agreed with his convention that assented to his desire to ordain Absalom Jones with this proviso: "Resolved that the same be granted, provided it is not to be understood to entitle the African Church to send a clergyman or deputy to the Convention or to interfere (sic!) with the general government of the Episcopal Church; this condition being made in consideration of their peculiar circumstances at present." Again, blacks could well add vulgar racism to the proven charges against the brothers Onderdonk, bishops of New York and Pennsylvania. There was also John Payne, first bishop of the church in Liberia. Payne, a white, was highly honored "for the long and valued services rendered the Church and in behalf of the race to whose service he had consecrated his life." Alexander Crummell, certainly our most eminent priest, who also served in Liberia at this time, speaks of the degree of prejudice brought by the bishop and missionaries from America to Africa.

It is from the public addresses of our black clergy that we can gain insight into the experiences of black Christians who, through their deep commitment to Christ and their loyalty to their church, surmounted any temptation to renounce baptismal vows or promote schism. These sermons could only be preached by them, for only they could understand and describe the nuances of the black experience in this particular setting. Others may express how they observe us, and even attempt to interpret that experience; but they can not possibly know how we value life within the church, and, at the same time, identify ourselves with our black brothers and sisters who are not a part of this communion.

If there are those of us today who seem to carp, admonish, complain, and fight in councils and synods because we are still dissatisfied with the quality of witness within the church, these sermons should remind us that we stand within a great tradition. If there are those who question the necessity of such a national body as the Union of Black Episcopalians, the priests who wrote the sermons clearly demonstrate why such a watchdog agency is still needed. These men are speaking to their times. Their language is authentic and unequivocal. The conditions to which they addressed themselves have passed in many cases, and we, taking advantage of hindsight, can think of other ways of dealing with problems they faced; but their spirit of uncompromising loyalty both to the church and to their people remains as a rich legacy. They stand within the total black religious experience as legitimate and worthy figures in the varied Christian spectrum. All churches have had to wrestle in their own ways with racism. I am convinced that as we honestly accept our victories and defeats and understand our common discipleship, we can march together as a great fellowship toward that free and just society we believe is God's will for all his people.

The selection of contributors had of necessity to be arbitrary. I have known of these clergy either through what must be called the oral tradition (for, as we have noted, there is little written about them) or through personal acquaintance. In trying to be impartial, I am certain that I have not invited some of my closest friends to be a part of this witness. Others from the past would have been included, but careful research has discovered no extant manuscripts. Even today, some who have been asked have admitted that they keep no manuscripts and could not, therefore, comply with the requirement that these sermons must have been preached. This probably guarantees fresh thoughts for their hearers, but leaves posterity the poorer.

The opportunity to read these and so many other sermons of our clergy who have through the years spoken to our needs and aspirations has been both inspiring and hopeful; inspiring, for it has evoked pride in the high character of our priests and prophets; hopeful, for it justifies our faith that in the Gospel of Jesus Christ all will come to know that we are citizens of the kingdom of righteousness, freedom, and peace. If we would "choose a text" for this book, surely it would be this: "Wherefore seeing we also are compassed about with so great a cloud of witnesses, let us lay aside every weight, and the sin which doth so easily beset us, and let us run with patience the race that is set before us, looking unto Jesus the author and finisher of our faith" (Rev. 12: 1, 2a).

Absalom Jones concluded his *Thanksgiving Sermon* with this poem by Michael Fortune. There is no extant information about the author, although it is assumed that he was a member of Jones's congregation.

NEW YEAR'S ANTHEM
Michael Fortune

I

To Thee, Almighty, gracious power,
   Who sit'st, enthron'd, in radiant heaven,
On this bless'd morn, this hallow'd hour,
   The homage of the heart be given!

II

Lift up your soul to God on high,
   The fountain of eternal grace,
Who, with a tender father's eye,
   Look'd down on Afric's helpless race!

III

The nations heard His stern commands!
   Britannia kindly sets us free,
Columbia tears the galling bands,
   And gives the sweets of Liberty.

IV

Then strike the lyre! your voices raise!
   Let gratitude inspire your song!
Pursue religion's holy ways,
   Shun sinful Pleasure's giddy throng!

V

From Mercy's seat may grace descend,
   To wake contrition's heartfelt sighs!
O! may our pious strains ascend,
   Where ne'er the sainted spirit dies.

VI

Then, we our freedom shall retain,
   In peace and love, and cheerful toil,
Plenty shall flow from the wide main,
   And golden harvests from the soil.

1

ABSALOM JONES

The Reverend Absalom Jones was born in slavery in Sussex, Delaware, on November 6, 1746. He was brought to Philadelphia in 1762, where he worked and purchased his freedom and, later, that of his wife. He and the Reverend Richard Allen, another freed slave, became lifelong friends and co-workers in their efforts to help the black people of Philadelphia develop into responsible and stable citizens. The Free African Society, of which they were founders, was the first instance of blacks in America organizing themselves for social and economic progress, and its work touched every area of the community's life. When blacks were ejected from St. George's Methodist Episcopal Church, the society organized the "African Church of Philadelphia." At its founding, it was allied to no denomination and had no particular doctrinal base. However, the congregation soon voted to establish such an affiliation to give it stability and to serve as a basis for financial support. Allen wrote, "There were two in favor of the Methodists, Rev. Absalom Jones and myself, and a large majority for the Church of England." Allen refused an offer to become an Episcopal priest, preferring to remain a Methodist. He founded the independent African Methodist Episcopal Church, and became its first bishop. Jones accepted the offer to become an Episcopal priest, and founded the first parish among black people, St. Thomas's. Although choosing different paths for encouraging religion among their people, both men remained steadfast in their friendship and common zeal. Absalom Jones died in 1818.

This sermon was preached in St. Thomas's Church, Philadelphia, on January 1, 1808, in thanksgiving for the abolition of the African slave trade.

A Thanksgiving Sermon

And the Lord said, I have surely seen the affliction of my people
which are in Egypt, and have heard their cry by reason of their
taskmasters; for I know their sorrows; and I am come down to deliver
them out of the hand of the Egyptians.... (Ex. 3:7-8)

These words, my brethren, contain a short account of some of the
circumstances which preceded the deliverance of the children of Israel
from their captivity and bondage in Egypt.

They mention, in the first place, their *affliction*. This consisted in
their privation of liberty; they were slaves to the kings of Egypt, in
common with their other subjects, and they were slaves to their fellow
slaves. They were compelled to work in the open air, in one of the
hottest climates in the world, and probably, without a covering from
the burning rays of the sun. Their work was of a laborious kind; it
consisted of making bricks, and travelling, perhaps to a great distance,
for the straw, or stubble, that was a component part of them. Their
work was dealt out to them in tasks, and performed under the eye of
vigilant and rigorous masters, who constantly upbraided them with
idleness. The least deficiency, in the produce of their labour, was
punished by beating. Nor was this all. Their food was of the cheapest
kind, and contained but little nourishment; it consisted only of leeks
and onions, which grew almost spontaneously in the land of Egypt.
Painful and distressing as these sufferings were, they constituted the
smallest part of their misery. While the fields resounded with their
cries in the day, their huts and hamlets were vocal at night with their
lamentations over their sons, who were dragged from the arms of their
mothers, and put to death by drowning, in order to prevent such an
increase in their population, as to endanger the safety of the state by
an insurrection. In this condition, thus degraded and oppressed, they
passed nearly four hundred years. Who can conceive of the measure
of their sufferings during that time? What tongue, or pen, can

compute the number of their sorrows? To them no morning or evening sun ever disclosed a single charm; to them, the beauties of spring, and the plenty of autumn had no attractions; even domestic endearments were scarcely known to them; all was misery, all was grief, all was despair.

Our text mentions, in the second place, that in this situation, they were not forgotten by the God of their fathers, and the Father of the human race. Though, for wise reasons, he delayed to appear in their behalf for several hundred years; yet he was not indifferent to their sufferings. Our text tells us, that he saw their affliction, and heard their cry; his eye and his ear were constantly open to their complaint; every tear they shed was preserved, and every groan they uttered was recorded, in order to testify, at a future day, against the authors of their oppression. But our text goes further. It describes the Judge of the world to be so much moved, with what he saw and what he heard, that he rises from his throne—not to issue a command to the armies of angels that surrounded him to fly to the relief of his suffering children—but to come down from heaven, in his own person, in order to deliver them out of the hands of the Egyptians. Glory to God for this precious record of his power and goodness; let all the nations of the earth praise him. *Clouds and darkness are round about him, but righteousness and judgement are the habitation of his throne. O sing unto the Lord a new song, for he hath done marvellous things; his right hand and his holy arm hath gotten him the victory. He hath remembered his mercy and truth toward the house of Israel, and all the ends of the earth shall see the salvation of God.*

The history of the world shows us, that the deliverance of the children of Israel from their bondage, is not the only instance in which it has pleased God to appear in behalf of oppressed and distressed nations, as the deliverer of the innocent, and of those who call upon his name. He is as unchangeable in his nature and character, as he is in his wisdom and power. The great and blessed event, which we have this day met to celebrate, is a striking proof that the God of heaven and earth is the *same, yesterday, and to-day, and for ever.* Yes, my brethren, the nations from which most of us have descended, and the country in which some of us were born, have been visited by the tender mercy of the Common Father of the human race. He has seen the affliction of our countrymen, with an eye of pity. He has seen the wicked arts, by which wars have been fomented among the different tribes of the Africans, in order to procure captives, for the purpose of selling them for slaves. He has seen ships fitted out from different ports in Europe and America, and freighted with trinkets to be exchanged for the bodies and souls of men. He has seen the anguish which has taken place, when parents have been torn from their children, and children from their parents, and conveyed, with their hands and feet bound in fetters, on board of ships prepared to receive them. He has seen them thrust in crowds into the holds of those ships, where many of them have perished from want of air. He has seen such of them as have escaped from that noxious place of confinement, leap into the ocean, with a faint hope of swimming back to their native shore, or a determination to seek an early retreat from their impend-ing misery, in a watery grave. He has seen them exposed for sale, like horses and cattle, upon the wharves; or, like bales of goods, in warehouses of West Indian and American sea ports. He has seen the pangs of separation between members of the same family. He has seen them driven into the sugar, the rice, and the tobacco fields, and compelled to work—in spite of the habits of ease which they derived from the natural fertility of their own country in the open air, beneath a burning sun, with scarcely as much clothing upon them as modesty required. He has seen them faint beneath the pressure of their labours. He has seen them return to their smoky huts in the evening, with nothing to satisfy their hunger but a scanty allowance of roots, and these, cultivated for themselves, on that day only, which God ordained as a day of rest for man and beast. He has seen the neglect with which their masters have treated their immortal souls; not only in withholding religious instruction from them but, in some instances, depriving them of access to the means of obtaining it. He has seen all the different modes of torture, by means of the ship, the screw, the pincers, and the red-hot iron, which have been executed upon their bodies by inhuman overseers.

Overseers, did I say? Yes, but not by these only. Our God has seen masters and mistresses, educated in fashionable life, sometimes take the instruments of torture into their own hands, and deaf to the cries and shrieks of their agonizing slaves, exceed even their overseers in cruelty. Inhuman wretches! though you have been deaf to their cries and shrieks, they have been heard in Heaven. The ears of Jehovah have been constantly open to them; he has heard the prayers that have ascended from the hearts of his people, and he has, as in the case of his ancient and chosen people the Jews, *come down to deliver* our suffering countrymen from the hands of their oppressors. He *came down* into the United States, when they declared, in the constitution which they framed in 1788, that the trade in our African fellow-men would cease in the year 1808; *he came down* into the British Parliament when they passed a law to put an end to the same iniquitous trade in May, 1807; *he came down* into the Congress of the United States, the last winter, when they passed a similar law, the operation of which commences on this happy day. Dear land of our ancestors! thou shalt no more be stained with the blood of thy children, shed by British and American hands; the ocean shall no more afford a refuge to their bodies, from impending slavery; nor shall the shores of the British West India island, and of the United States, any more witness the anguish of families, parted forever by a public sale. For this signal interposition of the God of mercies, in behalf of our brethren, it becomes us this day to offer up our united thanks. Let the song of angels, which was first heard in the air at the birth of our Saviour, be heard this day in our assembly. *Glory to God in the highest, for these first fruits of peace upon earth, and good-will to man.* O! let us give thanks unto the Lord, let us call upon his name, and make known his deeds among the people. Let us sing psalms unto him and talk of all his wondrous works.

Having enumerated the mercies of God to our nation, it becomes us to ask, What shall we render unto the Lord for them? Sacrifice and burnt offerings are no longer pleasing to him; the pomp of public worship, and the ceremonies of a festive day, will find no acceptance with him unless they are accompanied with actions that correspond with them. The duties which are inculcated upon us, by the event we are now celebrating, divide themselves into five heads.

In the first place, let not our expressions of gratitude to God for his late goodness and mercy to our countrymen be confined to this day, nor to this house; let us carry grateful hearts with us to our places of abode, and to our daily occupations, and let praise and thanksgiving ascend daily to the throne of grace, in our families, and in our closets for what God has done for our African brethren. Let us not forget to praise him for his mercies to such of our colour as are inhabitants of this country, particularly for disposing the hearts of the rulers of many of the states to pass laws for the abolition of slavery, for the number and zeal of the friends he has raised up to plead our cause, and for the privileges we enjoy, of worshipping God, agreeable to our consciences, in churches of our own. This comely building, erected chiefly by the generosity of our friends, is a monument of God's goodness to us, and calls for our gratitude with all the other blessings that have been mentioned.

Secondly, let us unite, with our thanksgiving, prayer to Almighty God, for the completion of his begun goodness to our brethren in Africa. Let us beseech him to extend to all the nations in Europe, the same humane and just spirit towards them which he has imparted to the British and American nations. Let us, further, implore the influence of his divine and holy Spirit, to dispose the hearts of our legislatures to pass laws, to ameliorate the condition of our brethren who are still in bondage; also, to dispose their masters to treat them with kindness and humanity; and, above all things, to favour them with the means of acquiring such parts of human knowledge, as will enable them to read the holy scriptures, and understand the doctrine of the Christian religion, whereby they may become, even while they are the slaves of men, the freemen of the Lord.

Thirdly, let us conduct ourselves in such a manner as to furnish no cause of regret to the deliverers of our nation, for their kindness to us. Let us constantly *remember the rock whence we were hewn, and the pit whence we were digged. Pride was not made for man,* in any situation, and, still less, for persons who have recently emerged from bondage. The Jews, after they entered the promised land, were commanded, when they offered sacrifices to the Lord, never to forget their humble origin, and hence, part of the worship that accompanied their sacrifices consisted in acknowledging that *a Syrian, ready to perish, was their father;* in a like manner, it becomes us, publicly and privately, to acknowledge that an African slave, ready to perish, was our father or our grandfather. Let our conduct be regulated by the precepts of the gospel; let us be sober minded, humble, peaceable, temperate in our meats and drinks, frugal in our apparel and in the furniture of our houses, industrious in our occupations, just in all our dealings, and ever-ready to honour all men. Let us teach our children the rudiments of the English language, in order to enable them to acquire a knowledge of useful trades, and above all things, let us instruct them in the principles of the gospel of Jesus Christ, whereby they may become *wise unto salvation.* It has always been a mystery, why the impartial Father of the human race should have permitted the transportation of so many millions of our fellow creatures to this country, to endure all the miseries of slavery. Perhaps his design was that a knowledge of the gospel might be acquired by some of their descendants, in order that they might become qualified to be the messengers of it, to the land of their fathers. Let this thought animate us, when we are teaching our children to love and adore the name of our Redeemer. Who knows but that a Joseph may rise up among them, who shall be the instrument of feeding the African nations with the bread of life, and of saving them, not from earthly bondage, but from the more galling yoke of sin and Satan.

Fourthly, let us be grateful to our benefactors, who, by enlightening the minds of the rulers of the earth, by means of their publications and remonstrances against the trade in our countrymen, have produced the great event we are this day celebrating. Abolition societies and individuals have equal claims to our gratitude. It would be difficult to mention the names of any of our benefactors, without offending many whom we do not know. Some of them are gone to heaven, to receive the reward of their labours of love toward us; and the kindness and benevolence of the survivors, we hope, are recorded in the book of life, to be mentioned with honour when our Lord shall come to reward his faithful servants before an assembled world.

Fifthly, and lastly, let the first of January, the day of the abolition of the slave trade in our country, be set apart in every year, as a day of public thanksgiving for that mercy. Let the history of the sufferings of our brethren, and of their deliverance, descend by this means to our children, to the remotest generations; and when they shall ask, in time to come, saying, What mean the lessons, the psalms, the prayers and the praises in the worship of this day? Let us answer them by saying, the Lord, on the day of which this is the anniversary, abolished the trade which dragged your fathers from their native country, and sold them as bondmen in the United States of America.

Oh thou God of all the nations upon the earth! We thank thee, that thou are *no respecter of persons,* and that thou *has made of one blood all nations of man.* We thank thee, that thou hast appeared, in the fullness of time, in behalf of the nation from which most of the worshipping people, now before thee, are descended. We thank thee, that the sun of righteousness has at last shed his morning beams upon them. Rend thy heavens, O Lord, and *come down* upon the earth, and grant that the mountains, which now obstruct the perfect day of thy goodness and mercy towards them, may *flow down at thy presence.* Send thy gospel, we beseech thee, among them. May the nations, which now sit in darkness, behold and rejoice in its light. May Ethiopia soon stretch out her hands unto thee, and lay hold of the gracious promise of thy everlasting convenant. Destroy, we beseech thee, all the false religions which now prevail among them, and grant that they may soon cast their idols to the moles and the bats of the wilderness. O, hasten that glorious time, when the knowledge of the gospel of Jesus Christ, shall cover the earth, *as the waters cover the sea; when the wolf shall dwell with the lamb, and the leopard shall lie down with the kid, and the calf and the young lion and the fatling together, and a little child shall lead them; and when, instead of the thorn, shall come up the fir tree, and, instead of the briar, shall come up the myrtle tree and it shall be to the Lord for a name and for an everlasting sign that shall not be cut off.* We pray, O God, for all our friends and benefactors, in Great Britain, as well as in the United States; reward them, we beseech thee, with blessings upon earth, and prepare them to enjoy the fruits of their kindness to us, in thy everlasting kingdom in heaven; and dispose us who are assembled in thy presence, to be always thankful for thy mercies, and to act as becomes a people who owe so much to thy goodness.

We implore thy blessing, O God, upon the President, and all who are in authority in the United States. Direct them by thy wisdom, in all their deliberations, and O save thy people from the calamities of war. Give peace in our day, we beseech thee, O thou God of peace! and grant, that this highly favoured country may continue to afford a safe and peaceful retreat from the calamities of war and slavery, for ages yet to come. AMEN. We implore all these blessings and mercies, only in the name of thy beloved Son, Jesus Christ, our Lord, and now, O Lord, we desire, with angels and arch-angels, and all the company of heaven, ever more to praise thee, saying, *Holy, Holy, Holy, Lord God Almighty; the whole earth is full of thy glory. AMEN.*

2

PETER WILLIAMS, JR.

Peter Williams, Jr., was the son of one of the founders of the African Methodist Episcopal Zion Church. His father, the senior Peter Williams, converted to Methodism while still a slave; he had been purchased by the trustees of the John Street Methodist Church in New York City to be the sexton. He, with James Varick, headed a group of blacks who successfully petitioned Bishop Francis Asbury in 1799 to form a separate fellowship of black Methodists "to exercise their spiritual gifts among themselves," and in the following years they built their "Zion" church. Peter Williams, Jr., followed his father in his concern for the religious well-being of the black community of New York. However, like the parting of Jones and Allen in Philadelphia, he also decided to leave his father's denomination and enter the ministry of the Episcopal Church. Like his father, he was an ardent patriot, and was convinced that under the "glorious Declaration of American Independence," his people would gain their freedom and become worthy citizens of the republic.

In 1818, Peter Williams, Jr., founded the great St. Philip's Episcopal parish in New York City, becoming its rector and the first black priest in that diocese. He was an outstanding civic leader and an active member of antislavery groups. He was particularly critical of the African Colonization Society, for he was convinced that many whites had as an ultimate goal the removal of all free blacks from America by returning them to Africa. Bishop Benjamin Onderdonk insisted that he refrain from this agitation on threat of expulsion from the ministry and the closing of his parish. To save both, he acquiesced.

This sermon, delivered at a Fourth of July observance, offers the suggestion that free Negroes wishing to leave the United States, rather than return to Africa, might go to Canada where many had already gone and were well received.

A Plea for Help

The festivities of this day [July 4] serve but to impress upon the minds of reflecting men of colour, a deeper sense of the cruelty, the injustice, and oppression, of which they have been the victims. While others rejoice in their deliverance from a foreign yoke, they mourn that a yoke a thousandfold more grievous, is fastened upon them. Alas, they are slaves in the midst of freemen; they are slaves to those, who boast that freedom is the unalienable right of all; and the clanking of their fetters, and the voice of their wrongs, make a horrid discord in the songs of freedom, which resound through the land.

No people in the world profess so high a respect for liberty and equality as the people of the United States, and yet no people hold so many slaves, or make such great distinctions between man and man. From various causes (among which we cheerfully admit a sense of justice to have held no inconsiderable rank), the work of emancipation has within a few years been rapidly advancing in a number of the states. The state we live in, since the fourth of July 1827, has been able to boast that she has no slaves, and other states where there still are slaves, appear disposed to follow her example.

These things furnish us with cause of gratitude to God; and encourage us to hope, that the time will speedily arrive, when slavery will be universally abolished. Brethen, what a bright prospect would there be before us in this land, had we no prejudices to contend against, after being made free. But alas! the freedom to which we have attained, is defective. Freedom and equality have been "put asunder." The rights of men are decided by the colour of their skin; and there is as much difference made between the rights of a free white man, and a free coloured man, as there is between a free coloured man and a slave. Though delivered from the fetters of slavery, we are oppressed by an unreasonable, unrighteous, and cruel prejudice, which aims at nothing less than the forcing away of all the free coloured people of the United States, to the distant shores of Africa. Far be it from me to impeach the motives of every member of the African Colonization Society. The civilizing and christianizing of that vast continent, and the extirpation of the abominable traffic in slaves (which, notwithstanding all the laws passed for its suppression, is still carried on in all its horrors) are no doubt the principal motives, which induce many to give it their support.

But there are those, and these are most active and most influential in its cause, who hesitate not to say, that they wish to rid the country of the free coloured population, and there is sufficient reason to believe, that with many, this is the principal motive for supporting that Society; and that whether Africa is civilized or not, and whether the slave trade be suppressed or not, they would wish to see the free coloured people removed from this country to Africa.

How inconsistent are those who say, that Africa will be benefitted by the removal of the free people of colour of the United States there, while they say, they are the *most vile and degraded* people in the world. If we are as vile and degraded as they represent us, and they wish the Africans to be rendered a virtuous, enlightened and happy people, they should not *think* of sending *us* among them, lest we should make them worse instead of better.

The colonies planted by white men on the shores of America, so far from benefitting the aborigines, corrupted their morals, and caused their ruin; and yet those who say that *we* are the most vile people in the world, would send us to Africa, to improve the character and condition of the natives. Such arguments would not be listened to for a moment, were not the minds of the community strangely warped by prejudice.

We are *natives* of this country; we ask only to be treated as well as *foreigners*. Not a few of our fathers suffered and bled to purchase its independence; we ask only to be treated as well as those who fought against it. We have toiled to cultivate it, and to raise it to its present prosperous condition, we ask only to share equal privileges with those who come from distant lands to enjoy the fruits of our labor. Let these moderate requests be granted, and we need not go to Africa nor anywhere else, to be improved and happy. We cannot but doubt the purity of the motives of those who deny us these requests, and would send us to Africa, to gain what they might give us at home. But they say, the prejudices of the country against us are invincible; and as they cannot be conquered, it is better that we should be removed beyond their influence. This plea should never proceed from the lips of any man who professes to believe that a just God rules in the heavens.

The African Colonization Society is a numerous and influential body. Would they lay aside their *own* prejudices, much of the burden would at once be removed; and their example would have such an influence upon the community at large, as would soon cause prejudice to hide its deformed head. They profess to have no other object in view than the colonizing of the free people of colour on the coast of Africa, *with their own consent.* It is very certain that very few people of colour wish to go to that land. The Colonization Society *know* this, and yet they do certainly calculate that in time they will have us all removed there. How can this be effected but by making our situation worse here, and closing every other door against us?

God in his good providence has opened for such of us as may choose to leave these States, an asylum in the neighbouring British province of Canada. There is a large tract of land on the borders of Lake Huron, containing a million acres, which is offered to our people at $1.50 an acre. The persons who have bargained for the land, have found it necessary to apply to the citizens of the United States to aid them by their donations in raising the amount necessary to make their first purchase; and to aid a number of emigrants who were driven away in a cruel manner and in a destitute condition from Cincinnati, to seek a home where they might, and who have selected the Huron tract as their future home.

The coloured population of Cincinnati were an orderly, industrious and thriving people, but the white citizens, having determined to force them out, first entered into a combination that they would give none of them employment; and finally resorted to violent measures to compel them to go. Should the anxiety to get rid of us increase, have we not reason to fear, that some such courses may be pursued in other places? Your brethren exiled from Cincinnati for no crime, but because God was pleased to clothe them with a darker skin than their neighbours, cry to you from the wilderness for help. They ask you for bread, for clothing, and other necessaries to sustain them, their wives and their little ones, until, by their industry, they can provide themselves the means of support. The poor were compelled to fly without delay, and consequently need assistance. Brethren, can you deny it to them?

I know you too well, to harbour such a thought. It is only necessary to state to you their case, to draw forth your liberality. Think then, what these poor people must have suffered, in being driven with their wives and their little ones, from their comfortable homes, late in the autumn, to take up their residence in a wide and desolate wilderness. O, *last* winter must have been to them a terrible one indeed. We hope that they, by their own efforts, will be better prepared for the next; but they must yet stand in need of help. They have the rude forest to subdue; houses to build; food to provide. They are the pioneers for the establishment of a colony, which may be a happy home for thousands and tens of thousands of our oppressed race.

O think of the situation of these your brethen whom the hand of oppression has driven into exile, and whom the providence of God has perhaps doomed like Joseph to suffering, that at some future day, *much people may be saved alive.* Think of them and give to their relief as your hearts may dictate. "Cast thy bread upon the waters: for thou shalt find it after many days" (Eccl. 11:1).

3

JAMES THEODORE HOLLY

James Theodore Holly was the first American black man to be consecrated a bishop in the Episcopal Church. He was born a Roman Catholic, but became a member of St. Matthew's Episcopal Church, Detroit, Michigan. He was ordained deacon there in 1855. He soon became known for his leadership in the black nationalist movement of his day. He was convinced that American blacks could achieve freedom only through a mass migration to Haiti, and he wrote and lectured prolifically on this subject. He became a national figure because of the brilliance of his address and his obvious dedication to this cause. Not content with oratory alone, he led a group from his own congregation, St. Luke's, New Haven, Connecticut, and from other New England and Canadian communities, to Haiti. Good intentions were almost destroyed by the ravages of tropical diseases, but he and a small group remained to establish a church, in a country largely Roman Catholic, that he considered Catholic, but free from papal authority.

The Episcopal Church invited this Haitian body to come under its jurisdiction, and, in 1874, Holly became its bishop. He labored arduously both for the development of his own diocese and for the welfare of his adopted country. He died in 1911, honored both by church and state.

The article included here is excerpted from one of several papers entitled "Thoughts on Hayti" that he wrote for the *Anglo-African Magazine* in 1859.

Thoughts on Hayti

The recent bloodless revolution through which Hayti has passed and which has resulted in the dethronement of Faustin I and in the elevation of Geffrard to the chair of the Chief Magistrate; together with the revival of the subject of Haytian emigration among colored Americans, have contributed to bring the claims of this negro nationality prominently before the public mind. I, therefore, propose to profit by the attention which is now being bestowed upon the affairs of that country, to furnish some food for the public mind, by exposing some of my own thoughts derived from a somewhat careful and extended study of the history of the Haytian people....

In the first place, let me say that the successful establishment of this negro nationality; the means by which its establishment was sought and accomplished; and the masterly vigilance by which the same has been maintained for upwards of a half-century, present us with the strongest evidence and the most irrefragable proof of the equality of the negro race that can be found anywhere, whether in ancient or modern times. Among all the nationalities of the world, Hayti stands without any question the solitary prodigy of history. Never before in all the annals of humanity has a race of men, chattelized and almost dehumanized, sprung by their own efforts, and inherent energies from their brutalized condition, into the manly status of independent, self-respecting freemen, at one gigantic bound; and thus took their place at once, side by side with nations whose sovereignty had been the mature growth of ages of human progress. The ancient glory of Ethiopia, Egypt and Greece, grows pale in comparison with the splendor of this Haytian achievement. Because civilization having grown to gradual maturity under the most favorable circumstances on the banks of the Ganges, rolled its slow length along until it penetrated into Ethiopia, and from thence following the course of the Nile passed into Egypt, and coursed onward into Greece; and finally has rolled its restless tide over Modern Europe and the Western world. But the people of Hayti, without the elevating influence of civilization among them; without a favorable position for development; without assistance from any quarter; and in spite of the most powerful combination of opposing circumstances, in which they found themselves, at times contending against the armies of France, England, and Spain; these people, I say, in the face of all these obstacles, aroused themselves to the consciousness of their own inherent dignity, and shook off from their limbs the shackles and badges of their degradation, and successfully claimed a place among the most enlightened and heroic sovereignties of the world. Such, in short, is the important position that Hayti holds when compared with the nations of all ages, past and present, that have figured in the world's history.

But this importance does not diminish in the least if we take a more circumscribed view of her relations. Let us confine ourselves to this continent alone and compare her with the nationalities of the New World. She is second on the list of independent sovereignties in the Western Hemisphere that have successfully thrown off European domination during the last 80 years. And if the United States can claim to have preceded her in this respect, Hayti can claim the honor of having contributed to the success of American Independence, by the effusion of the blood of her sable sons, who led by the gallant Rigaud, a man of color, fought side by side with the American heroes in the Battle of Savannah. And, if since her independence, her government cannot claim the same stability of administration as that of the United States and Brazil, yet she can claim to have been far superior in this respect to all the Hispano-American nationalities that surround her.

Hence, then, with this living, breathing nationality rearing its sovereign head aloft over the Caribbean sea; and presiding as the Queen of the Antilles, we need not resort to any long drawn arguments to defend negro-Ethnography...in our day. Let [opponents] prove, if they can, to the full satisfaction of their narrow souls and gangrened hearts, that the black faced, woolly haired, thick lipped and flat nosed Egyptians of Ancient times did not belong to the same branch of the human family that those negroes do, who have been the victims of the African Slave-trade for the past four centuries....

From these thoughts, it will be seen that whatsoever is to be the future destiny of the descendants of Africa, Hayti certainly holds the most important relation to that destiny. And if we were to be reduced to the dread alternative, of having her historic fame blotted out of existence, or that celebrity which may have been acquired elsewhere by all the rest of our race combined; we should say preserve the name, the fame, and the sovereign existence of Hayti, though everything else shall perish. Yes, let Britain and France undermine, if they will, the enfranchisement which they gave to their West Indian slaves by their present Apprenticeship system; let the lone-star of Liberia, placed in the firmament of nationalities by a questionable system of American philanthropy, go out in darkness; let the opening resources of Central Africa be again shut up in their wonted seclusion; let the names and deeds of our Nat Turners, Denmark Veazeys, Penningtons, Delanys, Douglasses and Smiths be forgotten forever; but never let the self-emancipating deeds of the Haytian people be effaced; never let her heroically achieved nationality be brought low; no, never let the names of her Toussaint, her Dessalines, her Rigaud, her Christophe and her Petion be forgotten, or blotted out from the historic pages of the world's history.

The vantage ground given us in the former cases can be dispensed with rather than in the latter, because the white race can claim credit for having aided us to attain thereto; and thus they have ground to say that without them we could not have made this advancement; they might still continue to argue that when left to ourselves, we retrograde into barbarism. But in the case of Hayti the question of negro capacity stands out a naked fact, as vindication of itself, not only without any aid whatever from the white man, but in spite of his combined opposition to keep down in brutal degradation these self-emancipated freemen. From this view of the matter it may be seen that if Haytian independence shall cease to exist, the sky of negro-destiny shall be hung in impenetrable blackness; the hope of Princes coming out of Egypt and Ethiopia soon stretching forth her hands unto God, will die out; and everlasting degradation become the settled doom of this down-trodden, long afflicted, and then God-forsaken race.

Therefore to despise the claims of Hayti, is to despise the cause of God, by which he promises to bring deliverance to the captives and to those who are bound; to be indifferent to these claims is to neglect the holiest duties that Providence imposes upon us; and to refuse to make any and every sacrifice to advance the interest and prosperity of that nation is to be a traitor both to God and humanity. Hence, then, let that tongue cleave to the roof of its mouth that would dare speak against her; and let that arm wither that would not be upraised to defend her cause, against a sacrilegious desecration by the filibustering tyrants of mankind, and the sworn enemies of God. And to this solemn prayer let every manly heart that beats within a sable bosom respond, Amen.

4

ALEXANDER CRUMMELL

The life and ministry of Alexander Crummell are well described in the address by Archdeacon Henry L. Phillips that is also included in this book. A moving tribute is paid to him by W. E. B. DuBois in his book, *The Souls of Black Folk*. The Union of Black Episcopalians has raised the possibility of his name being included in the "Commemorations" in the Book of Common Prayer. He is worthy of such recognition, for he continues to stand for the best that blacks have contributed to our national life in church and society. His strength of character, his religious commitment, and his constant advocacy of freedom and justice are the marks of a modern Christian saint and hero.

The Race Problem
in America

The race problem is a moral one. It is a question entirely of ideas. Its solution will come especially from the domain of principles. Like all the other great battles of humanity, it is to be fought out with the weapons of truth. The race problem is a question of organic life, and it must be dealt with as an ethical matter by the laws of the Christian system. "As diseases of the mind are invisible, so must their remedies be...."

It is to be observed in the history of man that, in due time, certain principles get their set in human society, and there is no such thing as successfully resisting them. Their rise is not a matter of chance or haphazard. It is God's hand in history. It is the providence of the Almighty, and no earthly power can stay it. Such, pre-eminently, was the entrance of Christianity in the centre of the world's civilization, and the planting of the idea of human brotherhood amid the ideas in the laws and legislation of great nations. That was the seed from which have sprung all the great revolutions in thought and governmental policies during the Christian era. Its work has been slow, but it has been certain and unfailing. In the early part of the eighteenth century this principle of brotherhood sprouted forth into a grander and more consummate growth, and generated the spirit of democracy.

When I speak of democracy I have no reference to that spurious, blustering, self-sufficient spirit which derides God and authority on the one hand and crushes the weak and helpless on the other. The democratic spirit I am speaking of is that which upholds the doctrine of human rights; which demands honor to all men; which uses the State as the means and agency for the unlimited progress of humanity. This principle has its root in the Scriptures of God, and it has come forth in political society to stay! In the hands of man it has indeed suffered harm. It has been both distorted and exaggerated, and without doubt it needs to be chastised, regulated and sanctified. But the democratic principle in its essence is of God, and in its normal state it is the consummate flower of Christianity, and is irresistible because it is the mighty breath of God.

It is democracy that has demanded the people's participation in government and the extension of suffrage, and it got it. It has demanded a higher wage for labor, and it has got it, and it will get more. It has demanded the abolition of Negro slavery, and it has got it. Its present demand is the equality of man in the State, irrespective of race, condition or lineage. The answer to this demand is the solution of the race problem.

In this land the crucial test in the race problem is the civil and political rights of the black man. The only question now remaining among us for the full triumph of Christian democracy is the equality of the Negro. Nay, I take back my own words. It is *not* the case of the Negro in this land. It is the nation which is on trial. The Negro is only the touch-stone. By this black man she stands or falls. If the black man cannot be free in this land, if he cannot tread with firmness every pathway to preferment and superiority, neither can the white man. "A bridge is never stronger than its weakest point."

> In nature's chain, whatever link you strike,
> Tenth or ten-thousandth, breaks the chain alike.

So compact a thing is humanity that the despoiling of an individual is an injury to society.

This nation has staked her existence on this principle of democracy in her every fundamental political dogma, and in every organic State document. The democratic idea is neither Anglo-Saxonism, nor Germanism, nor Hibernianism, but *humanity,* and humanity can live when Anglo-Saxonism or any class of the race of man has perished. Humanity anticipated all human varieties by thousands of years, and rides above them all, and outlives them all, and swallows up them all!

If this nation is not truly democratic then she must die! Nothing is more destructive to a nation than an organic falsehood! This nation cannot live—this nation does not deserve to live—on the basis of a lie! Her fundamental idea is democracy; and if this nation will not submit herself to the domination of this idea—if she refuses to live in the spirit of this creed—then she is already doomed, and she will certainly be damned. But neither calamity, I ween, is her destiny.

The democratic spirit is of itself a prophecy of its own fulfillment. Its disasters are trivialities; its repulses only temporary. In this nation the Negro has been the test for 200 years. But see how far the Negro has traveled this time. In less than the lifetime of such a man as the great George Bancroft, observe the transformation in the status of the Negro in this land. When Bancroft was a child the Negro was a marketable commodity, a beast of the field, a chattel in the shambles, outside of the pale of the law, and ignorant as a pagan. Nay, when I was a boy of 13, I heard the utterance fresh from the lips of the great J. C. Calhoun, to wit, that if he could find a Negro who knew the Greek syntax he would then believe that the Negro was a human being and should be treated as a man. If he were living today he would come across scores of Negoes, not only versed in the Greek syntax, but doctors, lawyers, college students, clergymen, some learned professors, and *one* the author of a new Greek Grammar.

But just here the caste spirit interferes in this race problem and declares, "You Negroes may get learning; you may get property; you may have churches and religion; but this is your limit! This is a white man's Government! No matter how many millions you may number, we Anglo-Saxons are to rule!" This is the edict constantly hissed in the Negro's ear, in one vast section of the land.... Yes, let everything go to smash! Let civilization itself go to the dogs, if only an oligarchy may rule, flourish and dominate!

We have a blatant provincialism in our own country, whose only solution to the race problem is the eternal subjugation of the Negro, and the endless domination of a lawless and self-created aristocracy. Such men forget that the democratic spirit rejects the factious barriers of caste, and stimulates the lowest of the kind to the very noblest ambitions of life. They forget that nations are no longer governed by races, but by ideas. They forget that the triumphant spirit of democracy has bred an individualism which brooks not the restraints of classes and aristocracies. They forget that, regardless of "Pope, Consul, King," or oligarchy, this same spirit of democracy lifts up to place and power her own agents for the rule of the world. They forget that, as letters ripen and education spreads, the "Sambos" and the "Pompeys" of today will surely develop into the Toussaints and the Christophes, the Wards and the Garnets of the morrow, champions of their race and vindicators of their rights. They forget that democracy, to use the words of de Tocqueville, "has severed every link of the chain" by which aristocracy had fixed every member of the community, "from the peasant to the king."

They forget that the Church of God is in the world; that her mission is, by the Holy Ghost, "to take the weak things of the world to confound the mighty," "to put down the mighty from their seats, and to exalt them of low degree"; that now, as in all ages, she will, by the Gospel, break up the tyrannies and useless dynasties, and lift up the masses to nobleness of life, and exalt the humblest of men to excellence and superiority.

Above all things, they forget that "the King invisible, immortal, eternal" is upon the throne of the universe; that thither caste, and bigotry and race hate can never reach; that He is everlastingly committed to the interests of the oppressed; that He is constantly sending forth succors and assistances for the rescue of the wronged and injured; that He brings all the forces of the universe to grind to powder all the enormities of earth, and to rectify all the ills of humanity on the day of universal brotherhood.

By the presence and the power of that Divine Being all the alienations and disseverances of men shall be healed; all the race problems of this land easily be resolved, and love and peace prevail among men.

5

HENRY LAIRD PHILLIPS

Archdeacon Henry L. Phillips was born in Jamaica, West Indies, in 1847. Dying in 1947, Archdeacon Phillips can truly be described as a man who gave every year of his century-long life to the service of his church. Generations of black clergy knew him as a strict administrator, zealous for the Gospel, demanding as much of himself as he did of those who were under his supervision. He was graduated from Philadelphia Divinity School and ordained in 1876. He served as rector of the Church of the Crucifixion, Philadelphia, and was appointed Archdeacon for Colored Work in the diocese in 1912. He organized several churches in the city, and became a leading figure in the civic and religious life of the area.

This address was delivered before the Negro Historical Society at the time of the death of Alexander Crummell. The archdeacon was introduced as "a gentleman who holds a unique position in this city because of his wide influence here and because of the respect and esteem in which he is held by all classes."

In Memoriam: Alexander Crummell

How are the mighty fallen,
and the weapons of war perished!
(2 Sam. 1:27)

Those are the words of one young man bewailing the death of another young man to whom he was passionately attached. Yonder on Mt. Gilboa, is young Jonathan, the heir apparent to the throne of Israel fighting bravely and manfully against the Philistines. He is smitten to the ground and dies together with his father and brothers. David, the friend of Jonathan, who has already been anointed to be king over Israel, forgets that honor, and in the sorrow of his heart exclaims, "How are the mighty fallen, and the weapons of war perished!"

When on the tenth day of September, death claimed for his own, Rev. Alexander Crummell, Doctor in Divinity, a mighty man fell and the weapons of war so far as his eloquent tongue and trenchant pen were concerned perished. He was a man of wonderful qualities. He had a commanding presence. He was a striking and convincing writer; an eloquent speaker, a fearless champion of his race and a delightful conversationalist.

Alex Crummell was born in New York, March 1819. He was the son of an African prince, stolen when a boy and brought to this country. His grandfather was king of Tenne, West Africa, a country adjoining Sierre Leone. His mother was a freewoman, born in New York State. In the days of his youth there was not a single college or seminary in the United States that would admit a black boy. They were days of deep darkness and tribulation for Negroes in this land. Proslavery and caste spirit dominated the country. Chief Justice Taney's statement that "The Negro had no rights which a white man was bound to respect," was but the common sentiment of the nation.

At an early age Crummell was taught reading and writing, and was sent to the Mulberry Street School [New York], taught by Quakers. Subsequently, in common with his sisters and brothers, he received further instruction from white teachers employed by his father. In 1831, a high school was established by the Reverend Peter Williams, Crummell's pastor, aided by his father, Mr. Thomas Downing, and other leading colored men, who employed a white teacher to give instruction in Latin and Greek. This school sharpened Crummell's appetite for larger facilities and culture. But alas! where could he and youth of a like mind . . . look? Not a ray of hope was discernible on the intellectual horizon of the country. "Fortunately, however, just at this time, in the year 1835, the abolitionists of New Hampshire, disgusted with the Negro hatred of the schools and mortified at the intellectual disabilities of the black race, opened a school at Canaan, New Hampshire. Youths of all races and sexes were to be received into it."

For this school, Henry Highland Garnet, Thomas S. Sidney and Alex Crummell started with the greatest possible delight. . . . It was a journey of about four hundred miles and rarely would an inn or a hotel give them food, and nowhere could they get shelter! And this in a Christian country! This among a people who had sought these shores to secure religious liberty. Hear Dr. Crummell himself:

> . . . sufferings from pain and exposure, sufferings from thirst and hunger, sufferings from taunt and insult at every village and town, and ofttimes at every farm house as we rode, mounted upon the top of the coach, through all this long journey. It hardly seems conceivable that Christian people could thus treat human beings through a land of ministers and churches. . . . But our stay was the briefest. The Democracy of the state could not endure what they called a "nigger school" on the soil of New Hampshire, so the word went forth . . . that the school must be broken up. On July 4th, with wonderful taste and felicity, the farmers assembled at Canaan and resolved to remove the academy as a public nuisance. On August 10th, they gathered together from the neighboring towns, seized the building, and with nine yoke of oxen, carried it off into a swamp about a half mile from the site. They were two days in accomplishing their miserable work.

The house in which Crummell and the other boys were, was attacked that same night and fired upon, but as Garnet replied by a discharge from a double-barreled shotgun, the cowardly ruffians did not stay. . . . Shortly after, information was received that Oneida

Institute, at Whitesboro, a Manual Labor Seminary, had opened its doors to colored boys. Thither young Crummell repaired and spent three years under the excellent instruction of Reverend Beriah Green. Mr. Crummell, having decided to enter the ministry of the Protestant Episcopal Church, determined to endeavor to get the best training possible, and yet at the same time he proposed never to submit to the degrading conditions under which Reverends Absalom Jones, Peter Williams and William Levington had entered it, viz.: "That they would never apply for admission to the conventions in the diocese in which they lived." He became a candidate for orders in 1837, and at once, under the direction of the rector, the Reverend Mr. Williams, of St. Philip's Church, New York, he applied for admission to the General Theological Seminary in New York.

Dr. Whittingham, afterwards Bishop of Maryland, was then Dean of the faculty. He received the candidate most graciously and said to him: "You have just as much right to admission here as any other man. If it were left to me you should have immediate admission to this Seminary, but the matter has been taken out of my hands . . . and I am very sorry that I cannot admit you." Mr. Crummell then drew up a petition to the Trustees of the Seminary asking for admission. It fell like a bombshell into the midst of that august body, causing the most intense consternation and exasperation. The Right Reverend George W. Doane of New Jersey was the only one who championed the cause of Mr. Crummell. The petition was rejected. Crummell himself says of the occasion: "Immediately during the session of the Trustees, Bishop Onderdonk sent for me and, then and there, in his study, set upon me with a violence and a grossness, that I have never since encountered, save in one instance in Africa. . . . " On every side there was almost universal anger against him. . . . Were there no others to champion the cause of humanity? Yes! There were a few. Even in Sardis, there were a few who had not defiled their garments. The honorable William Jay and John Jay, Esq., son and grandson of the illustrious John Jay, the first Chief Justice of the United States, Charles King, Esq., editor of the *New York American* and the Reverend Manton Eastburn, Rector of the Church of the Ascension, protested most vigorously against the action of the Trustees and the conduct of the Bishop. These gentlemen advised Mr. Crummell to go to Boston. They gave him letters to their friends. One introduced him to Reverend William Croswell, Rector of the Church of the Advent. Reverend Mr. Croswell was not only a

Divine, but a sweet poet deeply interested in the Negro race. While he could not personally do much for Mr. Crummell, he directed him to go to Reverend Dr. Vinton and the Reverend Mr. Clark. The Reverend Thomas M. Clark—now the venerable and aged Bishop of Rhode Island, was then a young priest, swaying by his inspiring eloquence and empyed character the crowds of worshippers who flocked to hear him.

Dr. Vinton, Reverend Mr. Clark and Reverend Mr. Croswell became the friends and patrons of Mr. Crummell. Through their influence he was introduced to the Venerable Bishop Griswold. The Bishop received him with fatherly interest and cordiality, and concluded his conversation with him by saying: "I wish there were twenty more of your race applying for orders. I should be more than glad to receive them as candidates for the ministry in this diocese...." " In Boston, he became a candidate for orders, and two years afterwards, May 1842, was ordained to the Diaconate, in St. Paul's Church in that city. In 1844, Bishop Lee of Delaware ordained him to the Priesthood. He began his ministerial labors at Providence, Rhode Island, but there he could not get support. From Providence, he came to Philadelphia. The Bishop of the diocese at that time was Right Reverend H. U. Onderdonk, brother of the New York Onderdonk. At the request of Mr. Crummell to labor here, the Bishop made the following reply, "I cannot receive you into this diocese unless you will promise that you will never apply for a seat in the convention for yourself or for any church you may raise in this city." Those who knew Dr. Crummell can well imagine what his answer to this iniquitous demand was: "That, sir, I shall never do...."

With but few exceptions, as in Providence, so in Philadelphia, the clergy would not support or recognize Reverend Mr. Crummell. He was looked upon as a disturber of the peace and must be punished by neglect. Not seldom reverend divines were rude and insulting to him. The result was poverty, want, sickness. He says of this period, "On one occasion I was in a state of starvation....

It was at this period of difficulty and darkness, when not enough colored people could be gathered together to build and support a church, that friends suggested that he should go to England, and appeal for funds to erect such a building. He reached England, January 1847, broken in health, but at the same time full of earnest purpose and brightest hopes. The letters which he carried soon brought him in contact with eminent persons both in the political and ecclesiastical world. His manliness and natural ability were soon seen and appreciated. His appeal for funds was kindly responded to.... His five years stay in England was a period of grand opportunities and richest privileges.... There probably has lived no other Negro who has been honored by personal contact and friendship with such a galaxy of stars of first magnitude. Dr. Crummell showed in his whole bearing not only the marks of a man who had graduated from Queen's College, Cambridge, but the marks of a man who had come into contact with the world's best and greatest. Having decided, on account of his health, to go to Africa, he landed in Liberia in 1853, and at once threw himself into the work of that young republic.... His missionary life was hedged up and crushed out by the malignant and caste spirit, in the bishop and many of the missionaries (white men, of course) which they carried from America, and which marred their own labors there.... He succeeded, however, in doing a healthful and elevating work.

Dr. Crummell believed, and believed rightly, that all people on their first passage from slavery to freedom need more rigidity. Having experienced the galling discipline of slavery, they need, as a correction to license, the "sober discipline of freedom." This is precisely what a new people cannot readily understand, and hence are always ready to oppose those who hold such principles. He was a teacher of morals. He stood on a high plain and shared the common fate of all moral reformers....

After living in Africa for nearly twenty years, he returned to the United States in 1873, and began work in the city of Washington, D.C. He founded St. Luke's Church, of which he remained Rector until he had accomplished fifty years of ministerial work. He resigned in 1895, and for awhile he was Rector Emeritus. He was the founder and president of the American Negro Academy. He was also president of the Colored Ministers' Union.

Dr. Crummell was buried from St. Philip's Church, New York, where his father was a vestryman; where he was a Sunday School scholar; where, under the influence of the Reverend Peter Williams, he had his mind towards the sacred ministry. He was an incessant writer for magazines, newspapers and other periodicals, besides being the author of several tracts. Whatever he wrote was eagerly read.... As the prophets of old are still speaking to us and influencing us through their writings, so will Dr. Crummell continue to do so. It was a pleasure to hear him speak. The eloquence of his diction, the felicity of style with which he expressed himself, the wide range of knowledge, the power to command that knowledge whenever wanted, showed the well-educated man and made him the center of attraction wherever he happened to be. Blood will tell. Dr. Crummell was the grandson of a king. He was a born ruler and could not brook opposition. This he showed in his whole manner and conversation. Dealing with a people who have not yet learned to submit gracefully to authority, when exerted by one of their own race, this trait of character, in Dr. Crummell often militated against his immediate usefulness. But it was that which made him a fearless champion of the race. He was no trimmer; he could not cringe; he would never bow to the storm, hoping in that way he would escape the fury; he would not accept work in any diocese under degrading conditions; he was always a fearless champion of the rights of the black man as *man*. He was a knight of which any race may well be proud. In the providence of God, he was raised up to do his mighty work, especially through the use of the pen, at the time when the Calhouns and others of that ilk were declaring that the Negro is not a man, or that if he could grapple successfully with the Greek verb, they would believe in his manhood.

The life, the hardships, the struggles of a man like Dr. Crummell should be known and studied by all the youths of the country. The difficulties that this man overcame in seeking an education, in entering the ministry, in fighting caste spirit, in battling with sickness, are as great, if not greater, as that which a Napoleon had to overcome in crossing the Alps in the winter. We are in the habit of reading about the one with bated breath, while we pass silently over the life of men like Dr. Crummell. Why? Because we have not yet learned to believe that moral courage is superior to physical.

He believed with Epictetus: "You will do the greatest service to the State if you should raise, not the roof of the houses, but the souls of the citizens; for it is better that great souls should dwell in small houses rather than for mean slaves to lurk in great houses."

6

GEORGE FRAZIER MILLER

George Frazier Miller, who served as rector of St. Augustine's Church, Brooklyn, for 47 years, was born in Aiken, South Carolina, in 1864. He attended Howard University, receiving his B.A., M.A., and D.D. degrees. He served churches in Charleston, South Carolina, and New Bern, North Carolina, before coming to Brooklyn. Known for his outstanding ability as a preacher, he was called upon in every section of the country to speak to college, religious, and civic groups. He was an active socialist, and was the object of much hatred because of his opposition to America's entry into World War I. In May 1909, he was part of a committee that prepared for the formation of the N.A.A.C.P., and, in 1919, with A. Philip Randolph, helped in the organization of the National Association for the Promotion of Labor Unionism among Workers. His death in 1943 brought to a close the life of a priest who always saw his ministry not only in terms of pastoral care of persons, but in the healing of a society that for him had alienated itself from the purposes of its Creator.

This sermon, delivered before a meeting of the Conference of Church Workers among Colored People, explains the Missionary Episcopate, a proposal to set the work among blacks under a black bishop in a "racial" rather than a geographical diocese.

The Missionary Episcopate as a Method of Evangelism

The universality of human dignity and the absoluteness of human worth is a fundamental principle of the religion of Christ. It is a primary Christian truth, and so instinctive is it in the demands of discipleship in the Lord Jesus that a rejection of this axiom is a preclusion from participation in the loftier things of God. He treads on quicksand who ventures abandonly upon the realm of dogmatising; still I make bold to say that they who despise, or affect to despise, their follow-men, are cursed with the disfavor of God though they exercise the highest authority in the militant Church of earth.

The clergy of this Conference have been contending for many years past, for due and proper recognition in the Church of their love. Into communion with the branch of the Holy Catholic and Apostolic Church of God, locally termed Prostestant Episcopal, we have come by the same natural, or normal, ways and means that others have entered her fold—by family ties, the proximity of the parish to our homes, the training of parochial schools, general association, the responsiveness of temperament and of mental insight to the Church's forms and teachings; and unless the Church be man-made, not God-ordained, we come by right, and not on the sufferance of men. Having come and seen the light as our Heavenly Father hath revealed it to the sons of men, we remain, as is our bounden duty and service, to receive of her divine bounties and to dispense her blessings to those to whom we humbly minister.

The Missionary Episcopate of colored people to colored people has been, with us, a crying demand for a considerable number of years. Some felt its need, most urgently, more than twenty-five years ago; and some have come to that position through many doubts as to propriety, or the soundness of ecclesiastical polity—the question of feasibility, the fear of ultimate schism, the unwillingness to see a canonical recognition of racial lines within the Church, and likely for many other reasons. These obstacles made the process to our present conviction not only a course fraught with vexing doubts, but a rugged path strewn with heartaches, engendering, at times, degrees of bitterness among ourselves as misunderstandings and disputations tend to do, however much we admire independence of thought, or heartily accede to individual liberty. But the attitude we now assume admits of no alternative. The question or color was interjected into the councils of the Church by others, not by ourselves; and the exigencies of the situation compel us to this defensive of self-respect.

Our clergy have not been slow to note these conditions and the significance thereof. Many of them have been manly enough to say in open court that the conditions are intolerable; that a normal development is impossible under such a regime, and nothing less than equality can be the determining element in a final adjustment: if you exclude us from diocesan conventions with all the rights and privileges inherent in their membership, then give us jurisdictions of our own wherein we may exercise the function of legislation and not be limited to spheres of petition.

When this demand is set forth—the only one compatible with self-respect—we hear the rejoinder: "Say we not well that you are black men, and are swollen with an overweening ambition?" When our Lord said, "Go not into the way of the Gentiles and into any city of the Samaritans enter ye not," He spoke as a devout Jew suffering His ministrations to be curtailed by the narrow confines of a covenant that "gendereth to bondage." But when the Old and decadent Testament with its circumcision and Sabbath became impotent and void upon the advent of the New Testament validated and evidenced in Holy Baptism and the Cup of the New Testament in His Blood, the universality of the Gospel mission—"Go ye into all the world" settled finally, the equality of all mankind in the things pertaining to God.

Like our Lord, we are careful not to enter any defence on the score of racial tie or class; but when we are told that we are devoid of the Christian grace of humility and are inflamed with an unholy ambition for place and power, we object to the charge and disclaim any such demoniacal possession. We assert, to the contrary, that we are actuated by the dictates of reason, the sense of propriety, and the recognition of the only course left to men earnest in their work, faithful to their trusts and longing to accomplish the best possible results for God and for man; but who labor now, unfortunately, under adverse conditions moulded by men of inimical minds. No priest of equitable mind would assume to exercise the prerogatives of a bishop, but no priest of virile temper will content himself with less than the privileges and powers usually accorded those of his own grade and office. That we should acquiesce in disfranchisement, and resign ourselves to the estate of pariahs and serfs in the Commonwealth of God, or in the civil privileges of our national life, we say *never,* so long as the Omnipotent One shall imbue our souls with the spirit of understanding, and enlarge our mouths with the power of protest.

In substitution of that for which we appeal, the suffraganate has been held out as a compromise of effective balm. Now a bishop suffragan is as worthy of esteem and deference as a diocesan bishop, though lacking in jurisdiction. But the suffraganate, at best, affords only the opportunity of petition and recommendation, precluding absolutely the power of initiative and decision inherent in the diocesan and missionary episcopate. The estate of a suffragan as per the scheme outlined in South Carolina would be an abomination and a reproach; and it is beyond the comprehension of some of us, if not all of us, how any man could so far be oblivious of his personal dignity and the exaltedness of the apostolic office as to kneel for consecration on such ignominious terms.

We do not say that the Missionary District as described and pleaded by our memorialists to the General Convention is a panacea or the indisputable and final state to be wished. We are not so bold as to lay down categorical imperatives of wisdom in the realm of human institutions and laws. We do say that, in view of the relations now subsisting between white and colored churchmen in the Southland, the establishment of the missionary jurisdiction is, in the light of our better judgment, a crying need, and therefore eminently worthy of the trial. We want to do a larger work, and are convinced of the need of modifications of the obtaining condition—the status quo—to an acceptable and efficient presentation of the Church to the masses of the people to whom our labors might be addressed. In the City of Washington, eleven years ago, the Reverend Professor Tunnell told our Right Reverend Fathers of the Southern States (between whom and ourselves there was a conference) very courteously, but nonetheless frankly, that the campaign in vogue seemed to be not so much "how to get the black man in, as how to keep him out."

The objection to our petition seems, in certain quarters, to be not so much to the plan proposed as to the personality of leadership. The Bishop of Nebraska, moved by our petition to the General Convention in Boston ten years ago, asked whether any colored man were qualified or fit to be a bishop. As the concept of fitness is a variant quality dependent for its determination upon ideals which, in turn, are fashioned by general environments, educational bias, and the development of the moral and aesthetic faculties, we cannot with certainty declare the fitness of any man. But if we base our assurance upon the criteria which have led white men of the American Church in their decisions—the manifest learning, integrity, sobriety, dignity without arrogance, lowliness without degradation, labors successful in the light of trammeling conditions, and alertness to serve men for Christ's sake—we ask the good bishop to look to his own diocese, in his own See City, and on the general clergy-list, in the neighborhood of his own honorable name. Of others we might make we desist.

From the earliest rumblings of unrest, when men began to discuss the advisability of some adaptation of the Historic Episcopate to the needs of the colored people, questionable motives and mental aberrations were imputed to us. In laying down the demands for a successful and gratifying prosecution of God's work in the harvest field, we are confident of bearing none of the distinctive marks of the demoniac, but prompted by a pure conscience, and, as we believe, a sound judgment, speak forth the words of truth and soberness. So, brethren, let us not despair—we are contending in a righteous cause—the cause of justice and truth. Imperfect though we are, still are we servants of God whose every work must bear the stamp of faith—faith deep-rooted and unswerving.

While claiming the liberty of unreserved expression on men and measures, we protest our loyalty to the Church of the living God, loyalty to the worship and discipline of the Book of Common Prayer, loyalty to the constitution and canons of the Church of our ordination. In honesty of purpose and integrity of soul, let all we do, be done; and striving for the right with all our might, let us labor in confidence that though men be suffered to ride over our heads, and we pass through fire and water, the God in whose hand our life is and whose are all our ways, will, in His gracious providence bring us out into a wealthy place.

7

KENNETH DEPOULLAIN HUGHES

Kenneth deP. Hughes was born in Grenada, West Indies, in 1902. He was graduated from the College of the City of New York and the General Theological Seminary, and served as rector of St. Mark's, Charleston, South Carolina, and St. Batholomew's, Cambridge, Massachusetts. At the time of his death in 1978, he was rector emeritus of St. Bartholomew's. His ministry was characterized by a constant and brilliant fight against injustice in society and racism in the church. He missed no opportunity to express his revulsion at any indication of oppression and prejudice, especially on the part of high officials, both political and ecclesiastical. His friendship with outstanding liberals made him the target of conservative activists, and he was called to testify before the Committee on Un-American Activities chaired by Senator Joseph McCarthy. He was ably defended by his bishop, Norman B. Nash of Massachusetts. He served as president of the Boston branch of the N.A.A.C.P., and was prominent in many organizations in the Boston area that worked for racial and economic justice.

This sermon is illustrative of his determination to use every occasion, even Easter, to denounce social evils. The community judged him to be a man who refused to "make peace with oppression."

Our Debt to the
Four Striking WACs

This Easter morning we make a radical departure from custom in the choice of a text. You will not find it in the Bible. We believe the Scripture contains all truths necessary for salvation, but we also believe that revelation is a continuing process. God speaks not only through priests and prophets, but also through simple people.

God spoke on March the tenth, 1945, at Fort Devens, Massachusetts, through four Negro privates in the Women's Army Corps, the WAC, court-martialed by the sixty-fourth Article of War. These four WACs provide us with our morning's text, and that is this: "We will take death if it will advance the cause of our people!" These four women are saying to us, "We are prepared to go through Good Friday if out of it will come new life, a resurrection from social death for an oppressed people—our people."

Two weeks ago, the whole nation, and this community in particular, were stirred by the unprecedented act of a strike by Negro members of the Women's Army Corps, at Fort Devens, who allege as cause for their act discriminatory practices by the officials of the United States Army. The outcome of this strike was trial by court martial of four of that number for violation of the sixty-fourth Article of War. I attended the trial. I heard the testimony pro and con. I spoke with the accused women. I want now to give you my reflections of it, not merely as it affects four colored girls who have been sentenced to prison, with dishonorable discharge, but what is infinitely more important, the implications of their act, and its inevitable repercussions throughout the nation. That it will advance the cause of an oppressed people I have no doubt. I pay tribute to their courage. If Easter means anything, it is this: no sacrifice made on behalf of a righteous cause can fail to bring forth good. It is in the very nature of the God we worship to make Easter follow inevitably upon each riday, no matter who is crucified. Both secular and religious history are back of these striking women.

Eighty-five years ago, a man stood on the gallows at Harper's Ferry, Virginia, and spoke these words: "I, John Brown, am now become fully convinced that the crimes of this guilty nation can never be washed away except by blood." One year later his words were proven true. And, nineteen hundred years ago, the author of the Epistle to the Hebrews wrote: "Without the shedding of blood there can be no remission of sins." Analogies from Scripture force themselves upon us. I see no difference in ideology between these striking women and that of Jesus Christ, as Saint Mark recounts, who steadfastly set his face to go up to Jerusalem, the danger zone, the city of martyrs, where he knew trouble awaited him, to lay down his life rather than budge a jot from his determination to achieve fair play and justice for all. It was he who first enacted, which was acted out, this principle of taking death to advance the cause of all mankind. It was this strong stand that made Easter possible. And if any race or group of people will have a resurrection to a life of self-respect, it must produce unflinching souls who say, "We will take death!"

Listen to the testimony of Frederick Douglass:

> He who is easiest whipped is oftenest whipped. I found that after resisting slave-master Coffee, I felt as I have never felt before. It was a resurrection from the dark and pestiferous tomb of slavery. I was no longer a servile coward, trembling...but my long coward's spirit was raised to an attitude of independence. I had reached the point where I was not afraid to die.

He, too, said, "I will take death!"

Let us briefly review the case. On March the ninth, 1945, colored WACs of a detachment at Ft. Devens went on strike. That is illegal. You cannot strike in the army. They refused to go back to work on the command of their superior officer, Col. Walter Crandall. He said he did not want any black WACs taking temperatures at Lowell General Hospital. They were to do the menial work. This same officer also told these strikers that he did not want any black WACs in the motor pool.

The four strikers were court-martialed on one specific charge: the violation of the sixty-fourth Article of War, refusing to obey a superior officer. The court was concerned only with the legality, not the morality, of the case. On legal grounds the Judge Advocate had a clear case against these four black women. There was much consideration shown. General Miles tried to be fair, insofar as anyone can be fair under a segregated setup, which is itself unfair. He told these women that no other members of the Army so offending had been given such consideration; and that was probably true. I got the feeling that these gestures toward leniency were the promptings of a guilty conscience. We lean over backwards toward those who have been wronged. They had a fair trial according to the rules. Two of the eight judges were Negroes. It would have taken but one other vote to get a hung jury. They were ably defended by Attorney Julian Rainey. But under the purely legal grounds upon which the case was tried, Rainey had no case. Everything was clear-cut against his clients. Open and shut. A prosecutor's paradise. I expected the verdict as rendered: Guilty! There could have been no other according to the rules. The sentence was lenient. It could have been death, and the four women knew it.

What then? Wherein lies the beneficence of their action? Was this some foolhardy act on the part of four simpletons flying in the face of providence and reason, or was it an act of calculated courage, a deliberate act for the liberation of their people? I think the latter is true, and for two reasons. First, these women knew what they were letting themselves in for, and they had a high unselfish motive: to advance the cause of their people. It was a voluntary self-offering on the altar of Negro freedom. They hoped, and as there is a just God, they will, by their vicarious sacrifice, bring to the attention of the whole nation the grievances buried deep in the hearts of Negroes everywhere, and which too seldom become recognized and made articulate.

In their cry, "We will take death!" is revealed the centuries-old hurt in the soul of the Negro. They spoke not for themselves alone, but for the fifteen million oppressed colored people throughout the land, who are saying the time is due, and overdue, to protest, and protest vigorously against the iniquitous conditions in the Army of the United States of America. They have thrown a challenge in the face of the status quo, and have served notice to the nation that colored people henceforth will not be ridden over roughshod and take it meekly. They have spoken for every Negro with red blood in his veins: "Give us the liberty that belongs to the children of God, or we will take death rather than live lives of slaves in a pernicious and oppressive system!" If the advocates of white supremacy can intimidate, they can subdue; but you can't intimidate a man who says, "I will take death!"

So, the handwriting is on the wall, writ in large letters so that all can read, accomplished by four gentle, unassuming black women, hardly out of their teens. It says that the days of white supremacy, which is no different from the Nazi doctrine of a superior race, are numbered. It can be weighed, and has been weighed in the balance, and found wanting.

The second cause for which we commend these four WACs is seen in the ethics of the case, which played no part in the trial. The armed services of our country are not concerned with "why" a soldier disobeys an order. He must do what he is told. And so, having disobeyed, the case against him is clear-cut. But no institution can afford to ignore morals and keep up morale. Let it then beware; men and women are not automata. They can stand but so much humiliation, and in the case of the black person, this humiliation has been going on for three hundred years. It reached its climax on March 9, 1945: that last straw was added when these nurses were told that no black WACs could take temperatures or join the motor pool. They must do the dirty work. The saturation point had been reached. The point at which tensions become unbearable. The hundred and one social mechanisms calculated to sap the Negro's manhood and place him on an inferior level. Somebody has got to say "No!" and these striking WACs said it. Alone, they balked the whole rotten system with a word that will go down in history. Our morning text: "We will take death to advance the cause of our people!" Amen.

8

MALCOLM G. DADE

Malcolm G. Dade was born in New Bedford, Massachusetts, in 1903, and received his education at Williston Academy, Lincoln University, and the Episcopal Theological School. He is now rector emeritus of St. Cyprian's Church, Detroit, Michigan, where he has served throughout his ministry. He has been active in diocesan affairs, serving as a member of the Executive Council, administrative assistant to Bishop Richard S. Emrich, and was the first black canon of the Cathedral Church of St. Paul, Detroit. Beyond ecclesiastical concerns, he has been a delegate to various international conferences, and was a member of the 1962 Michigan State Constitutional Convention. He was founder and first president of the Michigan Chapter of the Union of Black Episcopalians. His outstanding work in behalf of Labor was rewarded by his being made an Honorary Member of Ford Local 600— UAW-CIO. He has received a D.D. degree from Wilberforce University.

This sermon is both a review of his own ministry in Detroit and a clear picture of the involvement of a congregation in the struggle for economic security a generation before the "civil rights" movement.

St. Cyprian's Looks Back and Looks Ahead

What should the church be doing in these troubled times? Our city is being burned down. Our people are being intimidated, beaten, arrested, killed. We see our children inflamed with hate, our elders frightened and discouraged. Militancy is growing like wildfire among us all. And what is happening to us here in Detroit is happening throughout the land. We are not surprised that a modern American Civil War is taking place. For the past decade we have seen our efforts for justice and equal rights thwarted by criminal gangs asserting racial superiority; we have seen our churches and homes bombed; decent citizens, calling for their lawful rights, have been set upon by dogs and police with cattle prods; we have seen little children killed while attending Sunday School and leaders of the highest merit thrown in jail. And even the great apostle of nonviolence lies dead by an assassin's bullet. Surely, we are not surprised that the reaction of our people is shown in a wild, aimless desperate protest of fire, pillage and rioting. And we know that the black church, fulfilling its ancient role among our people, is deeply involved. So, I ask again, what is the nature of our involvement?

So far as St. Cyprian's Church is concerned—I say this carefully and deliberately—the answer comes easily: Do what we have been doing for the past thirty years! Identify with our people; be where they are; be willing to be hurt, to be misunderstood, to be denounced and falsely judged. Bear witness to our conviction that we have upheld through the years that the Christian Gospel speaks to the oppressed, the hurt, the distraught. The Gospel can speak through us to Detroit!

It is important that we review the story of our ministry here at St. Cyprian's. It is important for the newer members of our fellowship that they understand our history. It is important for the older members to recall the history of which they were a part. I tell this story, knowing full well my indebtedness to my own family, and the faithful members of the parish family who bore with me, supported me, suffered with me, often when we disagreed and misunderstood one another. We confess that we were not of one mind, and many feared for the future of our beloved church. But under grace, we discovered our mutual ministry and were able to forge ahead in the bonds of love.

Thirty years ago, St. Cyprian's was a little mission church on this West Side of Detroit. It was a congregation quite satisfied being small, dependent and clubby. In other words, it was like too many Episcopal churches in our Negro communities. But we had one great advantage—we were young and had no old customs and practices to live down! Much to the consternation of some old Detroiters, we were not of a mind to die, as some hoped, but really wanted to make our mark on the city. We decided that if we were going to grow to be effective witnesses we had to accomplish three things: We had to grow in numbers; we had to cease being dependent on diocesan handouts; and we had to direct our attention from ourselves to the needs of the city. We did all three: We presented again and again large Confirmation classes to the Bishop; we became an independent parish; and, you will surely understand from our remarks this morning, we went out into the city. Beyond these aims, we were the means of establishing three new Episcopal congregations, and we have seen several of our men enter the Church's ordained ministry.

My ministry among you started during the days of Depression and War. Our folk were employed, if at all, by the Ford Motor Co. and other auto plants. They were unorganized, ill-paid and uncertain of their jobs. The servicemen especially were afflicted by demeaning tasks and attitudes daily. United cooperative action was the only road to relief. I welcomed the efforts of union organizers to enter the Ford plant, even though it meant bloody beatings, intimidation—even death. Remember, you who are appalled by what is going on around us today, Detroit has suffered for the cause of social justice before! In fact, it was worse in those days, because the community was not united in the fight. Pastors of the largest churches in the Negro community were in the pocket of Ford. Their members owed their jobs to an autocratic paternalism; the churches were the recipients of generous, but tainted, gifts. In our struggle to swing public opinion behind us, for example, we invited Dr. Mordecai Johnson to come to speak and encourage us, and little St. Cyprian's had the only pulpit open to him. Mr. R. J. Thomas, the first president of the UAW-CIO Union honored me and this parish by giving me an honorary membership in the Ford Local 600, the largest local in the United Automobile Workers.

The victorious fight at the Ford plant set the tone of our future ministry. With the general economic improvement of our condition through union job security and better wages, the Negro population turned its attention to housing. It no longer wished to be confined to the traditional ghetto. We are now, of course, spread throughout the city and suburbs, but such a condition did not come, I assure you, without a fight. The National Association for the Advancement of Colored People, spurred on by our own Gloster Current, called for the united action of the whole city, and, of course, St. Cyprian's was there. Again, there appeared the police swinging clubs and now trampling us with their horses. There were the brave women and men walking the picket lines in all kinds of weather. There was the terrible expense of lengthy court cases. But thank God, the Community was now united. Never before had we experienced such unselfish, brave and generous response from our people. It was our Detroit housing case under the leadership of Thurgood Marshall and the N.A.A.C.P. that went to the U.S. Supreme Court. And the favorable results of that case broke open the neighborhood convenants and benefitted our people throughout the country. Most of you are living in homes that came to you as the result of this significant fight.

Whether we fought job discrimination, housing restrictions or police brutality, the people of Detroit were led by men and women who had truly a religious commitment to the cause of civil rights. We recall their leadership with pride and gratitude and pray God that people of like character will rise up to fight our way to freedom today.

Some may raise the question about why St. Cyprian's became involved in this way. I don't have to be reminded that the question was raised when we began, and has been raised throughout the years. Were we the Church, or just social activists? We have been accused by clergy and people of "playing politics," or of "getting out of the church's business." We said then, and we say now, that we tried to follow in the steps of the Master who went about doing good (Acts 10:38). His ministry of healing, of exorcism, of helping had to be interpreted according to our own understanding of our people's needs, who were being destroyed by the demons of power, prejudice and exploitation. We believe it is still the Church's task in carrying on this ministry to raise up those who fall, to care for the poor and fight those conditions that make and keep them poor, to proclaim the truth that sets all of us free.

We were always careful to keep our priorities straight. Because we cared for our own people, we found we must care for others. Because we loved our children, our love had to spill over into the welfare of other children. Because we were drawn to the beauty of our worship, we sought to make life outside our church building beautiful as God intended it to be.

If judgment is to come upon us, let it be the judgment of One who sits upon the throne and says, "Inasmuch as ye have done it unto one of the least of these..." (Mt. 25:40). Having been on our knees, and having received His Body and His Blood, in the name of God let us go into the streets and make common cause with the brethren!

9

TOLLIE LEROY CAUTION, SR.

Born in Baltimore in 1902, Tollie L. Caution was nurtured from birth in historic St. James's Church under the tutelage of its great rector, Dr. George Freeman Bragg. He was graduated from Lincoln University and the Philadelphia Divinity School, from which schools he also received honorary doctorate degrees. He has done graduate work at the University of Pennsylvania, and served parishes in Maryland, Pennsylvania, and New York. His pastorates were distinguished by remarkable work in liturgics and choral music. He served as successor to Bishop Bravid Harris in the office of Secretary for Negro Work in the National Council of the Espiscopal Church from 1945–1952, and in 1953, he became assistant director in the department of Domestic Missions. In both capacities Caution became so well acquainted with the work of the church among blacks that he is regarded as the chief source of our knowledge of the church's mission in this field.

It is the opinion of many black church people that Dr. Caution was the victim of a new kind of racism. Many whites who are regarded as liberal by their associates assume that they know more about "dealing with blacks" than blacks do themselves. Integrated organizations are often beset by whites who take for granted that they will exercise leadership in determining policy and strategy. This attitude seemed to be prevalent in the national office of the Episcopal Church. Although Dr. Caution had the confidence of his fellow black church people, it was the impression of many that his experience was not respected by his superiors, and decisions were made in his area of concern without consulting him. In 1957, it was not surprising when he asked for early retirement from this untenable situation.

This sermon reflects not only his appreciation for his fellow clergy in their work in the black community, but especially his knowledge of the work in the diocese of Pennsylvania.

.

Let Us Now Praise
Famous Men

In this year of 1976 we are celebrating the bicentennial of this country's independence. Philadelphia is the cradle of that great emancipation. This service today is the first of four services to be held here in 1976. It is a service of thanksgiving for the participation of black people in the Episcopal Church and community within the last 200 years. It is a service of thanksgiving for the departed black clergymen in the diocese of Pennsylvania who have served God in the churches here within the last 200 years. Their evening has brightened in the golden west. And God has called these faithful warriors home to rest.

In the Apocryphal Book of Ecclesiasticus, chapter 44, we find these words: "Let us now praise famous men, and our fathers that begat us."

Dr. Carlton Hayden, in his book *Struggle, Strife and Salvation*, relates the role of blacks in the Episcopal Church before the Declaration of Independence. He points out that the Episcopal Church in the United States came to be identified with the well-born, the educated and the rich. In the colonial period it was the first to declare the Gospel to Africans in what is now the United States and it baptized them as early as 1624. In 1701, an organization was formed in England called "The Society for the Propagation of the Gospel in Foreign Parts." Its purpose was to evangelize blacks and the American Indians.

Because the Episcopal liturgy necessitated the ability to read and write, it also necessitated teaching the black slaves. Between 1702 and 1783, over 309 mission clergy and teachers from England taught the blacks. With the coming of the Revolutionary War and its aftermath, the "society" was withdrawn from the United States. It left but a handful of blacks worshipping in various white parish churches. By this time blacks had absorbed much of European culture, religion, education and morality. Gradual abolition of slavery took part in the North, and with it came the rise of self-conscious black communities. Membership of blacks in the Episcopal Church declined.

Absalom Jones was ordained in St. Thomas's Church, here in Philadelphia, September 15, 1795. He used his church not only for worship, but also in the quest of black people for freedom, manhood and their physical as well as their spiritual welfare. The character of his ministry has continued the same unto this day. The history of black Episcopalians, with the assistance of white churchmen, would unite both races in a new fellowship and challenge racist America to conform to God's requirement of dignity and justice for all.

Since the ordination of Absalom Jones, many black priests have followed in his train. Today we lay upon God's altar the names of those men who, having finished their course in the ministry in this diocese, are now gathered to their Heavenly Father. We thank God for their lives and inspiration. Would that we could tell of the work of each and every one of them. Fourteen of their number pastored St. Thomas's, Philadelphia. Of these, certainly I can be pardoned if I mention one who was known, respected and loved actually by generations of churchpeople, here and abroad. I speak, of course, of Archdeacon Henry Laird Phillips. He was the greatest Roman of them all. His work is all about us. I know of no black man in our Episcopal ministry who founded and nurtured so many new churches, kept alive the older churches and was a father in God to more black ministers. He was a good overseer, a real Episcopos. His work extended to helping found great institutions for the betterment of the black community: churches, hospitals, schools, summer places for recreation, even a bank. He strove valiantly in the church for the acceptance of blacks as equals. The *Church Advocate* of June 1925 had this to say of him on the fiftieth anniversary of his ordination to the priesthood:

> Rev. Dr. Phillips has spent his entire ministry in the City of Brotherly Love. But while Philadelphia has been the center of his sphere of operation, his voice has gone out into all the world.... We yield high praise to God that the church in which we claim sonship is able to present to the world, as an example, a character so luminous, effulgent and fruitful in all good works for the Master. And we pray God that all of us may continue to strive to attain whither he has successfully led the way.

Archdeacon Phillips indicates to the church how black clergymen in this diocese have distinguished themselves as priests in spite of obvious difficulties. They have conducted their parishes without crudeness or ugliness. In general, they have been cultured, refined, educated persons. They have had a concern for the welfare of people without patronage or condescension. If we face the facts of life honestly and squarely, we must admit that our church has had a greater appeal to middle-class black people. White people generally have not been willing to deal eye to eye with this class. They have been much more at ease scattering crumbs to the poorer, underprivileged, unchurched blacks, because they would seldom have to approach them on either a social, educational or cultural level.

Many Negroes in America have in their blood and training some of the finer things of both races. We all have a heritage. The movement of black awareness bids the Negro or colored man to find his heritage in Africa. It is satisfying to look with pride on our background, for it is more than just an emotional experience. The fact of our heritage is not ours. We are not responsible for it. Besides our African past, even before emancipation, there were those of our people who served as cooks, butlers, barbers, maids, etc. Observing the best things in life, they adopted them for themselves, and passed these cultured qualities on to their children and their children's children. And the Episcopal Church has had many of these people, even though their true value was not recognized generally.

Langston Hughes wrote well of the aspirations of black Americans:

> I, too, sing America.
> I am the darker brother.
> They send me to eat in the kitchen
> When company comes.
> But I laugh, and eat well, and grow strong.
> Tomorrow I'll sit at table
> When company comes.
> Nobody'll dare say to me,
> "Eat in the kitchen," then.
> Besides, they'll see
> How beautiful I am.
> I, too, am American.

The men we memorialize today generally were men of culture, educated men with great conviction and strong personalities. They never stooped to gutter tactics to accomplish their goals for evangelization. They attempted to raise people up without descending to a lower level of thinking and acting. They were leaders in the truest sense of that word. They had been taught and had definite standards in worship, preaching, parish administration and public affairs. Yet, they did not use these assets as gimmicks to win favor. The diocese of Pennsylvania has an enviable record of the work done among black people by black clergy and laypeople.

However, this diocese has, to date, never elected a black bishop. It was not because there were no blacks qualified to be a bishop. On the contrary, perhaps it was because some were too qualified to be a suffragan bishop, or perhaps too dynamic and aggressive to be the Diocesan Bishop of Pennsylvania! But we are not discouraged. If there is any sense of failure, let it be among those whose racism is stronger than their commitment to the Gospel. Our witness for these 200 years has been steadfast, courageous and faithful. We will not become the evil that we deplore. We are responsible for what is *now*, and what *shall be*. Many chains are still to be broken; many shackles still to be unfastened. As Paul Laurence Dunbar wrote:

> Go on and up, our souls and eyes
> Shall follow thy continuous rise;
> Our ears shall list thy story
> From bards who from thy root shall spring
> And proudly tune their lyres to sing
> Of Ethiopia's glory.

[Therefore] Let us praise famous men, and our fathers that begat us. The Lord hath wrought great glory by them through his great power. Leaders of the people by their counsels, and by their knowledge of learning. Meet for the people, wise and eloquent in their instructions. There be of them that have left a name behind them (and were the glory of their times) their praises might be reported. These were merciful men, whose righteousness hath not been forgotten. Their bodies are buried in peace, but their name liveth for evermore. The people will tell of their wisdom, and the congregation will show forth their praise. (Eccles. 44:1–15)

10

NATHAN WRIGHT, JR.

Nathan Wright was born in Shreveport, Louisiana, in 1923, and educated in the public schools of Cincinnati, Ohio. He has attended St. Augustine's College, the University of Cincinnati, the Cincinnati Conservatory, Ohio University, Temple University, West Virginia State College, the Episcopal Divinity School, Harvard Divinity School, and Boston State College, having received five earned degrees and numerous other honors. An activist as well as an academician, he served as field representative for the original CORE, and in 1947 participated in the first modern Freedom Ride testing the laws regarding interstate travel. While executive director of the department of urban work in the diocese of Newark, Dr. Wright was chairman of the historic 1967 National Conference on Black Power, and of the International Conference on Black Power in Philadelphia in 1968. He has served as rector of St. Cyprian's Church, Boston, and as chaplain in several institutions in the Boston area. He is the author of more than fifteen books, of numerous scholarly articles, and of two weekly commentaries on public policy issues in more than one hundred white and black newspapers. He is professor of urban affairs at the State University of New York at Albany.

The address included here was delivered in the Abyssinian Baptist Church, New York, and is a significant statement of his philosophy of self-help approaches to empowerment and economic development. As chief editorial consultant to Black Resources, Inc., and as originator of "Greater Things" ministries, Wright is advocating this emphasis through secular and religious channels.

Self-Development
and Self-Respect

When I was a child, I spake as a child,
I understood as a child, I thought as a child:
but when I became a man, I put away childish things.
(1 Cor. 13:11)

The central concern of the current issue of Black Power—for the good of the Negro and for the larger good of this whole nation and of our world today—is the self-development and the growth into maturity of the black people of America. Black people have been the sleeping giants of this land. Among all Americans, their power, insights and experience, potentially ready to enrich this nation, have been least developed. In words of cosmic import which speak to black people in uniquely immediate terms, "we have not yet become what we shall be."

The black people of America are this nation's most rich and ready asset—its greatest raw material—as once the unmined earth and its untouched forests, fields and rivers were. In former years this nation built its greatness upon the utilization, not unmixed with wastefulness, of the vast physical resources which had lain untapped. Today, the new frontier of this nation's destiny lies in the development and utilization to the full of its infinitely greater human resources. What greater and potentially more useful reservoir of undeveloped and unutilized human resources does this nation have than in the black people of this land?

The great difficulty which we have had in coming into our own in America has only, in these recent days of impetus toward Black Power, begun to be made plain. We have operated, for at least the last crucial period of thirty years, on the assumption that Negroes needed to be led into their wanted place of maturity in American life. This assumption should perhaps have been seen to be fictitious on its face. It is simply naive to believe that any person or any group of people may grow into maturity save in terms of their own self-development. As Dr. Adam Clayton Powell has repeatedly emphasized from this pulpit and elsewhere, human growth cannot be produced from without: it must always be developed from within. Thus, to the undoubtedly divine accident of the current focus on Black Power, black boys and girls, and black men and women—long lulled into a feeling of functionlessness and little worth—are awaking to realize that only through self-development can they become the people of power and of majesty and of might which their bearing the image of their Creator has destined them to be.

There is, on the part of the Negro, a manifest need for self-development. Yet, of recent years, we as black people have assumed that a slave mentality of dependence upon others, as we had in former years, was appropriate for the twentieth-century destiny to which we are called. This crippling dependence upon others has hung like an albatross on our necks. It has led us to the state of stagnation which we find, with a few notable exceptions, pervading the life of the black people of America today.

The experience of all rising ethnic groups in this our beloved land has been that each rising group in American life must do for itself that which no other group may do for it. Each rising group has had to devise, to engineer, and to control in its own way its own plan, however crude or inept it may seem to have been, for its own particular growth into freedom, into self-development, into self-sufficiency and into self-respect.

This path of self-development has been—since the well-known rejection by the American people in 1776 of the King George Plan for Coionial Development—the one and only truly American way. There has never been in the American experience a German-American plan for Jewish development. Nor has there been in the American experience a Polish plan for Italian development. Yet the black people of America have been led to believe that their due fulfillment and their appropriation of their due inheritance in America could come best, or even only, from a white American plan for black freedom. This is incongruous on its very face. The issue of Black Power for black people—and for the good of American people as a whole—speaks to the need for black people to move from the stance of humble and dependent and impotent beggars to the stature of men who will take again into their own hands, as all men must, the fashioning of their own destiny for their own growth into self-development and self-respect. Now herein lies precisely the singular difference between the impetus toward Black Power on the one hand and what we have known as the civil rights movement on the other.

While the civil rights movement has emphasized what black people have been due, the emphasis of black self-development is on what black people may give to America. The thrust of Black Power is toward national fulfillment through the utilization of the potentialities and latent gifts of all. Both Black Power and the civil rights movement must have their vital and necessary places. The civil rights movement has in its own invaluable way emphasized what the American Negro has been due as an American from the day of each black man's birth. Without the efforts of the civil rights movement, particularly over these past thirty and more years, it would be difficult to speculate on where we, and this nation as a whole, might be. The civil rights movement, with its interracial dialogue, needs to grow and to flourish. We must never indulge in the vain luxury of criticizing what our leaders—with the aid of others—have done for us in the past.

In the past we have needed help; and we have received it. But we lacked even more the fundamental necessity of self-help, and self-initiative. It is by this alone we as a people may grow into that self-direction and self-sufficiency which is incumbent upon all who would claim respect due to responsible and mature men. It is by black self-development that this nation may come most fully into its own. The absence of black self-development has taxed the resources of the nation and limited the national destiny. Black Power means black development into self-sufficiency for the good of Negroes and for the good of the whole nation. We want—as others must want—to replace the helping hand which now aids us with our *own* hand—to sustain ourselves and not be burdens on all others.

Black self-development means something more, as well. It means that we want to put into glorious use the latent resources that we have for devising new ways of bringing fulfillment to all life. From our position of powerlessness we have learned that only through an immediate and equitable extension of power can the white and black poor of our land be transformed from crippling liabilities into tangible assets. Poverty will begin to be abated most effectively when the particular and precious insights of black people are used in devising antipoverty efforts.

Black self-development also means that we as black people must take the initiative—using the brainpower and the other resources of all, under our own leadership—in building black unity, black pride and black self-confidence for the larger good of this whole nation. A strong, independent press oriented to the needs of black people will help us to achieve this. Black people have much to give to America. But it is only as black people first have confidence, pride and self-respect that they can give to America the rich gifts which it needs and must demand of us.

Undoubtedly, the most crucial part of black self-development is the building of our self-respect. We must see in ourselves nothing less than the image of God. Of all Americans, the black people of this land are by far the most intensely loyal. No one has ever questioned this. We are the unique products of our native land; and in every respect—for good *and* for ill—we have sought to emulate and to fulfill all that is American. In this endeavor, we have even gone so far as to adopt the white disdain for all that pertains to blackness. The sad fact is that in America black people have been taught that to be like other Americans they must come to hate themselves. Negroes are culturally conditioned to see themselves as childlike, immature and powerless. But the Scriptures tell us that we must love God with all our hearts and our neighbors *as ourselves.* How can we love our neighbors when we do not love and respect ourselves?

No one can instill pride and self-respect in another person. The same is true with ethnic groups. Every ethnic group, like every family, devises means of instilling group pride. Each idealizes its past and glorifies its ventures. So must the black people of America do. Instead of hating ourselves—as any group which dwells on its weaknesses does—we must accentuate the positive aspects of who and what we are. Every Negro in America must come to grow each day in self-esteem and self-respect. We need to have pride in ourselves. No one may give this to us. It is a matter of self-development. This task is our burden and ours alone as the central task, as the main business which is before us. This we must accept and aggressively and forthrightly implement not only for our needed self-respect, but also for the respect and acceptance of others, which must inevitably follow upon our growth into self-esteem and into self-respect.

This nation needs us, as does our world. We must take our hats from our hands, and we must stand on our feet. The old, if we but open our eyes to see it, has passed away. The new day is at hand. We must put away childish things, and assume the proud demeanor of men. So again the subject of our text: "When I was a child, I spake as a child, I understood as a child, I thought as a child: but when I became a man, I put away childish things" (1 Cor. 13:11). Amen.

11

AUSTIN RELLINS COOPER, SR.

Austin Cooper was born in Miami, Florida, in 1933, and received his education at St. Augustine's College and the Seabury-Western Theological Seminary. He had further study at the Cleveland-Marshall Law School. He has worked in Florida, Texas, New York, and Ohio. He is presently rector of St. Andrew's Church, in Cleveland, Ohio. His concerns for problems in the black community have been outstanding. He has served as president of the Cleveland branch of the N.A.A.C.P., and is active in the Masonic Lodge (Prince Hall Affiliation). His interests have gone far beyond the local parish in that he has been president of the national Union of Black Episcopalians, and has been a delegate to the 1974 consultation of the Anglican Church in the Province of Tanzania, and a member of the Episcopal Church's delegation to the Anglican Council of North America and the Caribbean.

This sermon was delivered in his parish church on the Sunday following the firing upon his rectory by a gunman who apparently objected to his civil rights activities.

God Is Trustworthy

And in the fourth watch of the night
Jesus went unto them, walking on the sea.
(Mt. 14:25)

The Gospel for today gives us the account of how our Lord showed himself to be indeed the divine ruler of nature and the comforter of the anguished souls of men. Having fed the multitudes, Jesus sent them away. This great throng of people had eagerly followed him—only to find themselves far from any place where they might purchase food. In their moment of confusion and bewilderment, he, the Son of God, showed himself to be good and kind and compassionate. In his presence men and women found themselves with food enough, and to spare. As he dismissed them, he gave his disciples instruction to get into a ship and to go over to the other side of the Sea of Gennesaret, and to wait there for him.

Nature is not always predictable. Nor is the Christian life and warfare. We begin the journey with relative ease and with high hopes, quite certain that we have more than it takes to be conquerors. The disciples did as Jesus commanded them. But about half-way across that body of water, the unpredictability of nature made itself felt with ungovernable fury! They soon discovered that they were in the midst of a sea which was churning, raging and furiously beating upon their small ship.

People who have been at sea in rough waters tell me that one is virtually defenseless, when nature's fury is unleashed. Many a well-constructed vessel has gone down, bowing in humble submission to a force greater than its own. It is not difficult, then, to understand how the disciples, there on a rough sea with darkness all around them, were fearful. Fearful of the elements! Fearful because Jesus was not with them! They found themselves, as our Lord's Church has so often been placed, and as every human soul has had to feel itself, far from shore and tempest-beaten. The rage of human foes is not so deaf, so brutal, so unmerciful, as the rage of wind and storm. It may be that Jesus wanted to test them, to see how they would stand up under the waves of life, which would seemingly engulf them as they proclaimed him Lord in every village and hamlet, every city and every town.

The disciples of Jesus—as do those who bear his name and sign today—found themselves out on a "stormy sea"! They had not thought about this aspect of discipleship. They had not understood that even to obey him is perilous. Yet Jesus knew that to obey him produces conflicts in our lives; that the waters, at times, can become turbulent; that the road can become rocky; that the mountainside can become rough; that the pathway can become thorny.

Our salvation comes in knowing that God does not forget us when He places us in life. "He who keeps Israel shall neither slumber nor sleep." God does not send us out into life without giving us the comfort of His loving and abiding presence. Jesus knew why he had sent the disciples out. He knew that the sea would become tempestuous. But he also knew that he would save them; that he had the capacity and the power to save them and all the people of God! God is able to do whatever must be done; including walking on the rough seas and making those rough seas and howling winds cease at his command! He is able to save you and me! If only our faith in his power and willingness to save does not weaken and falter. And even when we, because we are much like those disciples at sea, feel that we are being overwhelmed by the sea of life itself, Jesus still walks on the water, in order that we might be rescued. So we need not fret about the long night, when daybreak seems not to come. We need not become unduly alarmed, when the sea becomes stormy. This is the way of discipleship. "This is the way the Master went. Should not his servants tread it still?" Centuries ago, the prophet Isaiah could speak to Israel the promises of God: "When thou passest through the waters, I will be with thee! When thou walkest through the fire, thou shalt not be burned."

Things have happened in recent days to test my faith. But I want you to know this morning that I do not plan to "curse God and die"! "My soul is anchored in the Lord"! I believe that "the Lord Himself is our keeper—so that the sun does not burn us by day, neither the moon by night." Each night a police car is stationed outside my home; but I am trusting in a higher power to protect us! (Though that of the police will help, mind you!) I believe that each night God, from His throne of glory, dispatches a legion of angels to keep watch over us—and over you, and you, and you!

Way, way back yonder in Egypt, on the night before He was to free them, God instructed Moses to have the children of Israel take the blood of lambs and to strike the doorposts of every Hebrew home with this blood; so that when the angel of death passed over, he would know that these homes were to be spared because His people dwelt in them. When the shots rang out late last night, Jesus walked on the sea of life and protected us from harm. God walks with and keeps His people! Wicked forces did what they know best how to do: operate furtively and cowardly. They came to my home, under cover of night, pointed the shotgun towards a living-room window and fired! I was sitting directly in the line of fire and would surely have been struck, had the shots come all the way through. Some of my critics in the N.A.A.C.P. said that they were just pellets! I'd like to know how I was supposed to know that? I do know that when someone fires a gun at you, you do not stop and ask, "Are they blanks or the real thing?"

What those cowards do not know is that long before I came to Cleveland, I was washed in the waters of Baptism, and that in our household every member wears the sign of the Cross of Christ indelibly sealed on his or her forehead; and that weekly we drink from that life-giving and life-sustaining Cup—lovingly and freely outpoured on Calvary! What those cowards do not know is that when their angel—not God's angel of death—passed over our home, God, because He is God and has all power, also said to their wicked angel, "Pass over that house and do no harm! In that house My people dwell!" And when the shots were fired, God, from His throne of glory, reached down and, with His marvelous right arm and outstretched hand, turned back those shots intended for this prophet of the Lord. On this day I can rejoice with the Psalmist, "If the Lord Himself had not been on my side, now Israel may say; if the Lord Himself had not been on my side, when men rose up against me, they had swallowed me up alive when they were so wrathfully displeased at me."

God grant that as we go about our various tasks this week, we will experience, because of our worship of Him this day, the richness and joy of His presence, His inexhaustible grace and love and mercy. May someone else, in turn, come to know Him, because they will have seen Him glowing in our lives.

"And in the fourth watch of the night Jesus went unto them, walking on the sea."

12

JOHN M. BURGESS

This sermon was delivered by the editor before a diocesan service commemorating the Reverend Absalom Jones, first black priest of the Episcopal Church. These services are organized by chapters of the Union of Black Episcopalians as a witness to the presence and mission of the Episcopal Church in the black community and in the life of the diocese. The first part of the address is omitted because it reviews the experience of Jones and Richard Allen in withdrawing from the white congregation, an event described earlier in this book.

The Character
of the Black Witness

*I saw all the oppressions
that are practiced under the sun.
And behold, the tears of the oppressed,
and they had no one to comfort them!*

(Eccles. 4:1)

It is important for us to appreciate just why it was thought feasible for blacks to separate, to gather themselves together as a people committed to Almighty God for worship and church organization. From bitter experience those free blacks in Philadelphia learned it was unwise to put their future into anybody else's hands. The fact that white Christians were so determined to *not* let them be absolutely alone was not because they loved to have blacks around. Certainly they wanted them to be apart, but not out of their control! When the Council of the Diocese of Pennsylvania voted to allow Absalom Jones to be ordained without the required knowledge of Greek and Latin, it did so with the specific condition that neither he nor his parish of St. Thomas would ever attend the council and attempt to do business. And the parish was kept out for seventy-five years. So it was in New York where St. Philip's was kept out of the convention for forty years. The Philadelphia Methodists refused to recognize the separate existence of Richard Allen's A.M.E. Church for twenty years. It took special pleading on the part of James Varick and his group of blacks in New York to have his A.M.E.Z. Church recognized. There are instances where black people stood in the aisles of their churches to prevent white preachers from taking over their pulpits. In Savannah, Andrew Bryan, trying desperately to establish a black congregation of Baptists, was subjected to whippings and imprisonment for daring to preach the Gospel to his own people. Yet, he and his following endured all this finally to be victorious and establish his Baptist congregation in Georgia.

The black Church, the black congregation, has stood as a bastion of freedom for the black community. It has been the rallying place for the sharing of grievances, for planning strategy for future progress, for inspiring race pride, for getting out the vote, for raising money for education, lawsuits, charity, bail bonds and scholarships. How many chapters of the National Association for the Advancement of Colored People have been begun in black churches! In the churches we have in the name of God received inspiration to persevere, to suffer, to sacrifice—even to die, if need be. And the dominant race has not liked this. That is why it has wanted to keep control of the churches; that is why slave states actually prohibited the teaching of the Christian religion to slaves, no matter what the Constitution said about the separation of church and state. That is is why certain states prohibited the assemblying of blacks without the presence of whites. That is why in our day our churches have been bombed, set on fire, vandalized. Black people, looking back to the Exodus of the Jews from Egypt, believe in the God of freedom, the God Who said we were made in His image and likeness, thereby giving us dignity and worth.

Under such tutelage, we cannot be satisfied having ourselves defined by others, having our rate of progress determined by others, having our destiny decided by others. Father Nathan Wright has written,

> Human growth cannot be produced from without; it must always be developed from within. The experience of all rising ethnic groups in this our beloved land has been that each rising group in American life must do for itself that which no other group may do for it. While pushing and participating in the absolutely worthwhile interracial programs in the field of civil rights, the black people of America ought long ago to have been addressing themselves to the far more basic business of the development *by* black people *of* black people *for* the growth into self-sufficiency and self-respect *of* black people. We have much to give to America. But it is only as black people have confidence, pride and self-respect that they can give to America the rich gifts which it needs and must demand of us.

And we would say the same in our relationship to the Church. We love the Church—its doctrines, its liturgy, its way of life, its fellowship. And it is because of this love for the Church that we want it to be truly the Church. Absalom Jones gathered his people together to develop their own potential, their own resources, by themselves, for he was tired of being thwarted because of his color, insulted, managed by people who had no interest in the black community but to keep it under their control. But he did not sever St. Thomas's from the main body. The parish waited several generations before it was taken into the convention, as a witness to the true character of the Body of Christ. To gain this truth, to appreciate this character, the white Church needed this parish even more than St. Thomas's needed it! St. Thomas's drew apart in order that Jones's people could gather together and develop their own resources in their own way, and contribute them to the body of the Church itself. The Church does us no favor by *allowing* us in. There is mutual benefit, sharing and fellowship as there should be in an institution that calls itself church, and not sect. What a contrast between that Philadelphia diocesan convention and the recent General Conventions of the Episcopal Church at Notre Dame and Houston! Could the prayers of those eighteenth-century black Episcopalians be more vividly answered than in the rising up of blacks from every section of the country demanding that the Church face the evil of racism honestly and bravely as it faced the twenty-first century?

I believe that the Union of Black Episcopalians has its roots in the efforts of Absalom Jones and Richard Allen to come to terms with and deal with racism within American Christianity. The union is not a body upholding racial segregation within the Church. Some may say that the fact it is an organization for black Churchpeople is a reverse form of discrimination. What if white Churchpeople met and blacks were excluded? They do. They meet, they worship, they make important decisions, they plan, they build budgets and spend money, they recruit, they honor, they promote—and blacks are nowhere around. There are still too many churches where blacks are not welcome, and black clergy denied access. Blacks are kept out of leadership positions in parish, diocese and national Church. Our laity, often extremely well qualified, are not invited or elected to positions of responsibility, our clergy are left dangling with little hope of advancement or recognition. If this condition is to change, it will not be by coming with hat in hand asking for favors. It will change when we as a united body demand that the Church be the Church, where there can be no distinctions, segregations or discriminations among us.

Finally, we must remind ourselves that we have not only a duty to be witnesses to the Church—we have an equal responsibility to witness to the black community. The deep and abiding friendship of Absalom Jones and Richard Allen, binding Episcopalian and Methodist into a dynamic unity, should remind us that all black Christians have a duty toward their community that must surmount all denominational barriers and loyalties. Our Oneness in Christ Jesus should be enough to undergird our common fight for freedom. We join even with secular groups in fighting for freedom from want, unemployment, ignorance, disease, crime, corruption, exploitation of our labor. But as Christians we fight for even more. We know that mere freedom to live well is not a guarantee of peace. The folk who have so much more than the poor of our ghettoes and our slums, are not necessarily happy and contented people. Our affluent neighborhoods have more than their share of mental breakdowns, suicides, drug addiction, alcoholism and family disasters, and all the other symptoms of a disordered life. We are not striving to share their brokenness!

The black churches have the united task of offering to our people the living Gospel of our Lord Jesus Christ. This is a message of One who himself was poor, who suffered both in body and spirit, who was despised, rejected, beaten and mobbed, who died at the hands of selfish, prejudiced, jealous enemies. It is the Church that can see that the battle is not only racism, nor prejudice, nor selfishness—it is sin in its most degrading form. If victory is to come, as St. Paul says, it is to come through our acknowledgment of Jesus Christ as the Lord of all life. He is the One who liberates—liberates ourselves from sin, liberates our world from the powers of darkness, liberates us to become the kinds of men and women God intends us to be, liberates us to enjoy the world that He has created and ever makes new. In all our contention over race and poverty and crime and prejudice, we in the churches must pray and work for that personal relationship with Jesus Christ, that we may become effective channels of His grace into the world. For this we have been set apart.

In our dealings with the Church as black communicants, we have certainly earned the right through our struggle both in the Church and in the wider community as well, to speak of this freedom that the Gospel promises. Surely the Christian Gospel is biased toward the poor and the oppressed. "Behold, the tears of the oppressed, and they had no one to comfort them." Surely Christ, as we have come to know Him, is the answer to that need. We have forged a faith that gathers certainly earned the right through our struggle both in the Church and in the wider community as well, to speak of this freedom that the Gospel promises. Surely the Christian Gospel is biased toward the poor and the oppressed. "Behold, the tears of the oppressed, and they had no one to comfort them." Surely Christ, as we have come to know Him, is the answer to that need. We have forged a faith that gathers up into victory the defeats, the trials and tribulations, the hopes and dreams for which all people aspire. Whether whites or blacks like it or not, the religion of the self-conscious black community has come through the fire of testing, into the glorious hope of all the children of God. If the Episcopal Church wants to be set on fire, if it wants a new outpouring of the Spirit, it doesn't have to seek it in so-called charismatic cults and odd religious practices. In the words of Booker T. Washington, "let down its buckets where it is"; let down its buckets into the sea of our religious experience and gain new insight into what the Christian hope is all about. Then we, with all other members of Christ's flock, can actually sing, "Nobody knows the trouble I've seen. Glory, hallelujah!"

Are we prepared to offer this contribution? Do we have the vision of Jones and Allen who refused to be thwarted and suffocated by a religion imposed upon them? If these men are to be more than historical figures, more than fond memories of a distant past, then catch their spirit, put away self-hate, put away shame of race and color. Go forth creatively into your communities, take on church and civic responsibilities. Stop wringing your hands in despair. Hear the cries of the oppressed calling for comfort, guidance and hope. Bring our people to Christ. And may the God of peace who brought again from the dead our Lord Jesus Christ, the great shepherd of the sheep, make you perfect in every good work to do his will, working in you that which is well pleasing in his sight. And to him be the glory, both now and evermore. Amen.

13

NATHAN D. BAXTER

Nathan D. Baxter was born in Coatsville, Pennsylvania, in 1948, and was reared in the Holiness-Pentecostal tradition. He served in the U.S. Army Medical Corps and won the Vietnam Cross of Gallantry with Palms. He was graduated from Elizabeth College and Lancaster Theological Seminary, and is presently in the doctoral program of that school. He was ordained to the priesthood in 1977 in St. John's Church, Carlisle, Pennsylvania, where he had served as a lay assistant. He is rector of St. Cyprian's Church, Hampton, Virginia, and has assumed many responsible duties in the diocese of Southern Virginia. He is rapidly gaining attention as an outstanding preacher and has identified his ministry with the religious and civic life of his community. He assisted in the formation of a chapter of the Union of Black Episcopalians in his diocese.

This sermon is a review of the life of Absalom Jones. He raises the opportunity that challenges black Episcopalians to bear witness to their particular ministry in the black community.

The Feast of Absalom Jones, 1979

The year is 1787. The season is autumn. The city is Philadelphia. The members of the Continental Congress are now on their way home, after having scrapped the Articles of Confederation and undertaken to write the Constitution of the United States. The framework included: a two-house legislature, a president, a national judiciary. And an article on taxation and representation that declared the Negro 60 percent of a person.

Not far away from where the Congress had met, this shameful mentality was being acted out at St. George's Methodist Church. Years later Bishop Richard Allen, founder of the African Methodist Episcopal Church, recorded the event. He wrote:

> A number of us usually attended St. George's Church in Fourth Street; and when the colored people began to get numerous in attending the church, they moved us from the seats we usually sat on, and placed us around the wall, and on Sabbath morning we went to church and the sexton stood at the door, and told us to go sit in the gallery. He told us to go, and we would see where to sit. We expected to take the seats over the ones we formerly occupied below, not knowing any better. We took those seats. Meeting had begun, and they were nearly done singing, and just as we got to the seats, the elder said, "Let us pray. " We had not long been on our knees before I heard a considerable scuffling and low talking. I raised my head up and saw one of the trustees, having hold of the Rev. Absalom Jones, pulling him off his knees, and saying, "You must get up—you must not kneel here." Mr. Jones replied, "Wait until prayer is over." "No, you must get up now, or I will call for aid and force you away." Mr. Jones said, "Wait until prayer is over, and I will get up and trouble you no more." With that he beckoned to one of the other trustees to come to his assistance. He came and went to William White to pull him up.
>
> By this time prayer was over, and we all went out of the church in a body, and they were no more plagued with us in the church.[1]

He became founder of the A.M.E. Church; and Absalom Jones became the rector of the first black Episcopal congregation—St. Thomas's African Episcopal Church, and the father of black Episcopalians. They succeeded in putting their stamp on history, especially on American religious history. Despite the distinct difference in their theology and sociology regarding American Christianity, Richard Allen and Absalom Jones remained intimate lifelong friends. Together they established community real estate and the first black insurance company. During the yellow fever epidemic of 1793, when over 5,000 died, together they formed the single most effective corps of nurses and burial teams, primarily through their churches. Through the establishment of the Free African Society, they effectively aided the emancipation of slaves and the protection of the rights of free Negroes. They petitioned Congress in 1800 to free slaves. They also wrote, published and distributed pamphlets promoting these various causes. In the most exemplary sense, Allen and Jones were the Fathers of the Black Church as the "visible" American institution we know today.

However, the tension that they faced of being black in America remains the same even until now. And it is often a painful tension—one of affirming for ourselves the American dream—yet, somehow, knowing that the cost of that affirmation could well be our dignity, the very soul of our blackness. The symbols of this dream are empty if one does not have his dignity. The words of Jesus ring eternally true: "Will a person gain anything if he wins the whole world but is himself lost or defeated?" (9:25. Good News Bible).

The culture shock of the sixties and early seventies was particularly hard for the middle-class generation to understand. This was especially true of the radical pronouncements of identity employed by their children, the proponents of that culture. It was not easy for them to accept the preference of "black" for "Negro," the preferring of an "Afro" or bush to a neat trim with a part on the side; the appareling of African garb in preference to a vested suit or a sorority pin. To many this was a personal affront. But for the young middle-class generation in transition, this was a radical, and perhaps even a desperate attempt to regain a sense of selfhood—a sense they believed they had lost amid the shelter of their quasi-symbols of success.

The noble success of the post-World War II Negroes in dealing with the terrible tension of being black and being American resulted in the building of a mirror world of white middle-class America. It was a world that, by necessity, excluded even the larger black community. But more importantly, it became the world which would shelter their children from the painful realities of what it meant to be black and American. These sheltered children in the fifties and sixties discovered the suffering of the *un*sheltered who shared their ethnicity. Somehow they also discovered that they shared their suffering. And so, both those who built shelters of a mirror world and those who gave radical and violent pronouncement of identity are victims of this same crisis of being American and being black. This dilemma was defined by W.E.B. DuBois as "twoness." He wrote, "One ever feels his twoness— an American, a Negro; two souls, two thoughts; two unreconciled strivings; two warring ideals in one dark body."[2]

Our Christian experience commits us to the view that there is no greater source of strength in the struggle for justice, equality and human dignity than faith in Jesus Christ. It is we who have somehow glimpsed the ancient and intriguing mystery of God in Jesus Christ; who have by faith tasted of the divine love and mercy; who have transcended Jesus as the fair Caucasoid European prince of medieval fantasy to discover the suffering servant, the crucified prophet of Nazareth, the present and risen Lord. And it is we who must seek continually the sustenance of that same Lord to be faithful in the trial and rejoicing of His mission, which is justice, equality and human dignity for all people.

Since the days of Absalom Jones, black Christians have found two basic ways to live out their commitment of this faith in relation to the American church. First, there are those who, following Richard Allen, have taken their unjust affliction as the basis for the founding of an exclusive ethnocentric tradition. They have deemed it necessary to confront injustice from a power base alien to the established church. Second, there are those who, despite their affliction and the oppressor's exploitation of the true religion, desire the catholic faith and tradition of the Christian Church. They love the beauty and dignity of the liturgy. They desire the faith expressed in the creeds and sacraments; they desire to draw upon the power of the Gospel through the witness of almost 2,000 years of king and pauper, freedman and slave, and saintly martyrs. They refused to aid segregation by the creation of their own ghettoes of theology and institution, no matter how noble such a venture might be. These stand ground within the system of the established institutions—standing at every closed door—standing with and upon Him who said, "Behold, I stand at the door, and knock. If any man will hear me and open, I will come in with him and sup" (Rev. 3:20).

This is the stand of Absalom Jones and his children, black Episcopalians. It is often a perplexing and discouraging stand. It has often put us on the brink of self-alienation from our rich heritage as black people. It is the stand that sometimes makes us the subject of scornful suspicion by other black Christians. And we are often the victims of the subtle, but relentless, tide of systematic racism within our own church.

To make this choice is not easy. The tension sometimes tempts us to narrow the catholic and apostolic character of our faith by making God black and angry—exclusively bound to our ethnicity. Countee Cullen, a Harlem Renaissance master, expressed well our frustration in his poem "Heritage":

> Father, Son and Holy Ghost,
> So I make an idle boast;
> Jesus of the twice-turned cheek,
> Lamb of God, although I speak
> With my mouth thus, in my heart
> Do I play a double part.
> Ever at thy glowing altar
> Must my heart grow sick and falter,
> Wishing He I served were black.
> Thinking then it would not lack
> Precedent of pain to guide it,
> Let who would or might deride it;
> Surely then this flesh would know
> Yours had borne a kindred woe.
> Lord, I fashion dark gods, too,
> Daring even to give You
> Dark despairing features where,
> Crowned with dark rebellious hair,
> Patience wavers just so much as
> Mortal grief compels, while touches
> Quick and hot, of anger, rise
> To smitten cheek and weary eyes.
> Lord, forgive me if my need
> Sometimes shapes a human creed.[3]

However, like the Apostle Paul's thorn in the flesh, there is a positive dimension to our tension. It reminds us that our choice of approach to

American Christianity and whatever cultural advantages we may experience do not change our precarious plight of being black in America. We must face the reality of our plight, and with integrity acknowledge the kindred character of our oppression.

Where do we begin to find an effective balance in our churches between the polarities of creating sheltered mirror worlds of white middle-class values, and a radical reverse racist mentality and theology that breeds the cancerous disease of hate already destroying our society?

I believe we have already begun. Our desire to come together today in the strength of our heritage, worship and fellowship is as solid a beginning as there can be.

Tonight we are concerned and concerted. We are inspired by the faith of Jesus Christ, realizing that our mission is actually his. This awareness has called us to this point of union for mutual nurture and identity in the struggle for equality. Tonight we are a union of black Episcopalians; and I believe that all the company of heaven rejoices with Absalom Jones for this gathering of his children.

---

1. Sidney Kaplan, *The Black Presence in the Era of the American Revolution 1770–1800* (New York Graphic Society Ltd., 1973), p. 81.

2. Carol V. George, *Segregated Sabbaths: Richard Allen and the Rise of Independent Black Churches* (New York: Oxford University Press, 1973), p. 167.

3. Countee Cullen, *On These I Stand: An Anthology of the Best Poems* (New York: Harper and Bros., 1947), p. 27.

14

JOHN HOWARD JOHNSON

John H. Johnson was born in Richmond, Virginia, in 1897, and received his education at Columbia University and Union Theological Seminary in New York City. After serving on the staff of the New York City Mission Society for six years, he began his outstanding ministry at St. Martin's Church in Harlem. Under his leadership this parish became the most significant urban ministry of any black Episcopal congregation in the country. Starting as a small mission church, within a short time it numbered a membership in the thousands. It became the church home of the increasing population of West Indians and Southerners who came to the city during the Depression years. Aware of the suffering of their people, and not content with the meagre and unrealistic gestures for relief on the part of the public authorities and the business community, Dr. Johnson joined with the black leaders of Harlem in the campaign to put black employees in the places of business in Harlem. For twenty-five years he was a chaplain in the New York Police Department, and served as a trustee of the Cathedral of St. John the Divine from 1947 to 1965. He retired as rector emeritus of St. Martin's parish in 1965, but has continued an active ministry in both church and community.

The sermon is taken from his book, *A Place of Adventure* (Seabury, 1955). It is the message of faith in God and confidence in the strength and courage of his people that has characterized Dr. Johnson's ministry and made St. Martin's the great witness to the power of the Christian Gospel among the struggling masses of the city.

Less than the Least

Unto me, who am less than
the least of all saints . . .
(Eph.3:8)

This address is based on Paul's confession of inferior status. He felt and was made to feel an outsider. In his own words he was "less than the least of the apostles." He was not one of the original twelve. Since there was no place in the hierarchy at Jerusalem, he went to the gentiles. But although his prestige was slight, he could reply truthfully to his challengers, "Are they ministers of Christ. . . . I am more; in labors more abundant; in stripes above measure, in prisons more frequent, in deaths oft."

Like Paul, the Negro in the United States is "less than the least." Like Paul he feels, and is often made to feel, an outsider. From the beginning his lot has been hard; in our many-peopled land, he is the poorest, the weakest, the burden-bearer, the "pilgrim of the night" in search of a home. Yet, like Paul, the Negro can make claim to "labors more abundant." Value, both personally and nationally, is to be reckoned in what we give to others, in how much more we give than what we receive. Yet how few people, in estimating the contributions of the Negro to our civilization, consider how much his unremitting toil, given without adequate reward, has meant in the amassing of our national wealth. The Negro has been neither a drone nor a parasite. He has paid his way.

In the realm of the less material things, he has given us the Negro spiritual. Born from the darkness of slavery, it is eloquent testimony that there is something in the heart of man that adversity cannot crush. A humor that amuses, but never hurts is proverbially associated with the race. And in the Negro's warm heart wells a spring of gentleness and patience that never runs dry. No people has endured the violation of their rights with the extraordinary good will of the

Negro. Like St. Francis, when life crushes him, he looks up and smiles.

Perhaps the chief contribution of the Negro is the unshakable loyalty, the ingrained spirit of service that is his. For, uncertain of his status and hard pressed as he may be, the Negro considers America his home. His affection for his homeland burns with a steady fervor. It is rather pathetic to observe the ardent efforts he puts forth to conform to customs and ways that he hopes will entitle him to full citizenship and general approval. A struggle has been going on for a long time to make the American dream of freedom, equal opportunity, and equal justice come to pass for all. In this struggle the Negro has aligned himself solidly with the forces working for this end; he has shown that he may be counted upon to take whatever action the conflict indicates.

And his loyalty and enthusiasm, particularly during our recent emergencies, have been recognized and rewarded. Negroes are now serving in all branches of the armed services, achieving higher rank than ever before. In government, members of the race have been promoted to positions of importance. In many labor unions there has been an encouraging integration, and the employment opportunities now open to Negroes and the general level of wages are better than ever before. Knowing full well that much of this economic advancement has come through jobs that are only temporary, they have tried to give a good account of themselves with the hope they will hold the gains they have made.

But this is not enough. It must be clear to all that America is now caught in a crisis which has quickened everywhere the tides of our national life. Democracy is no longer a word that we may let fall complacently from our lips. It is now an idea for which we, or those we love, have fought and died. Everywhere issues emerge with greater clarity and deeper urgency. Everywhere people are clamorous; everywhere people are intense, and the Negroes are no exception. If we view the matter as a whole, we must conclude that Negroes have been long uncomplaining and cheerful under their burdens. But adverse conditions of long duration, irritating and unnecessary provocations make for a growing impatience that may express itself overtly in speech and action, or latently in slumbering resentment.

The fact of the matter is that the color bar continues to exist as a divisive faction in many areas of our national life, and it is of one in particular that I should like to speak now. The American Church, instead of leading in the fight against segregation, as it should, often falls in at the rear. No denomination or sect is entirely free from guilt in this respect. Despite the vigorous, unequivocal, and sincere public utterances of many of our bishops and other leaders who uphold in its fullest import the Christian doctrine of the brotherhood of man, nevertheless separation and segregation still prevail in many churches and in organizations under church control, such as hospitals, schools and rest homes.

This is true in practically all sections of the country where colored people live in appreciable numbers. An impenetrable veil, an iron curtain, seems to fall between the races, keeping them apart. No matter how clearly it is indicated or how urgently needed, any step forward in the matter of racial justice is taken only hesitantly, after it has been tried out somewhere else and found safe. Thus, instead of leading in the march toward brotherhood, the Church follows with lagging steps.

It is my belief that this cultural lag is the result of certain stereotypes of thought held even by well-meaning people, people who consider themselves Christians. There is first of all the idea, deeply embedded, that colored people are not the equal of white people and can never be, although the individual excellence shown here and there by certain members of the former group entitles them to a cordial, if somewhat condescending, acceptance by the latter. Then there is also the idea which many warm friends of the colored people entertain, that they are a child race, naturally destined to occupy always the place of servants in this world. Both of these ideas are as unscientific as they are unchristian. They make true brotherhood impossible, and are a denial of our Lord's teaching.

There is also what has been called the "theory of self-determination," accepted by many people who are deeply concerned with the problem of race relations. This theory can be summed up briefly in the following words: The dark races are inevitably set apart by skin pigmentation. They are races in the making. They have a destiny to fulfill and a rich contribution to make. They can do this, and will, if left to themselves and allowed to develop naturally under God.

The answer to this conveniently simple approach to what is one of the most complex and challenging problems of our times is that, while it is true that every race has its own destiny and its own contribution to make and while all racial and national groups will normally seek out their own kind and cling to each other, this inclination toward homogeneous group association in no way justifies policies of ostracism, unbrotherly attitudes, and the forcing upon minority groups of an inferior status.

That any person who thinks himself a Christian should be guilty of any of these attitudes is particularly reprehensible. For Christianity makes of fellowship as much an end in itself as communion with Christ. Paul admonished, "Above all these things put on charity, which is the bond of perfectness" (Col. 3:14). This charity, *agape* in Greek, is the love which the Son brings from the Father to mankind. It is the essence of fellowship, and, if truly embraced, as Paul says, it is "the bond of perfectness."

What a pity that the rare gifts that the Negro is able to bring now to the fellowship of Christians are not being received! For in this land there is deep spiritual need, hunger of soul. We need not struggle, as St. Paul did, "against beasts at Ephesus." Nobody bothers to stone the missionaries any more. But there is something more deadly with which we have to contend—apathy, indifference, a growing deafness of heart to the voice of God, and insulation of the spirit.

The Negro can help in this struggle. He has always been possessed of a glowing, ardent, unshakable faith. Even when he is poorly educated, he is deeply familiar with the Bible and the Book of Common Prayer and often expresses himself eloquently in their cadences. Used reverently over the years, these books have helped to nurture him, to feed his mind, to mould and strengthen his character, and to uplift his spirit.

He emerges with a strong faith in God, in man, and in life itself, a faith that makes it possible for him to endure with equanimity and patience, even with good cheer, the difficulties he faces day by day. How could he bear the cloud of circumstance which hems him in, if he did not see beneath it the silver lining of the love of God?

What great gifts, then, the Negro has to bring to our tired world! We shall be blessed as we try to build up the brotherhood, substituting understanding for ignorance, fellowship for estrangement. Our Lord left us the incentive: "Inasmuch as ye did it unto the least of these my brethren, ye did it unto me."

15

JUNIUS FLEMING CARTER, JR.

Junius Carter was born in Catonsville, Maryland, in 1927, and received his
education at St. Augustine's College and the Philadelphia Divinity School.
He has been pastor of churches in New Jersey and Pennsylvania, and, since
1966, has been rector of the Church of the Holy Cross, Pittsburgh. He is a
member of the Executive Council of the Episcopal Church. He has been
prominent in the efforts to fight racism both in the civic and religious life of
the communities in which he has served. He is a forthright speaker, hedging in
no way to express his judgment on any who are guilty of prejudice and
racism. As a deputy to the General Convention he has been vigorous in his
advocacy of programs for racial justice.

This sermon expresses his confidence that the church must be the vehicle
for social redemption.

God's Call to Unity, Love and Service

*Grace be unto you, and peace, from God our Father,
and from the Lord Jesus Christ. I thank my God
always on your behalf, for the grace of God which
is given you by Jesus Christ.*

I greet you in these familiar words of St. Paul when he spoke through his Epistles to the several Churches. I choose these words deliberately in these troubled times when so many things are happening to test our faith and challenge our beliefs. We are surrounded by violence, hatred, disorder, lack of regard for discipline, destruction, not only of material things, but of God's highest Creation, human life. Many of us had settled down into our comfortable complacency, allowing ourselves to believe that things were not really as bad as the "radicals" were telling us, and would get better if we just were patient.

Conditions did not improve, but grew steadily worse, and we are now seeing the result of man's inhumanity to man.

The late sixties and early seventies have marked the coming together of many black organizations and, above all, the coming together of the black Church—clergy and laity—unity in the face of adversity. From this unity we hope to achieve courage in the face of fear; restraint in the face of violence; order in the face of chaos and, above all, faith in the face of unbelief.

It has always been my belief that only when we once again make the Church the center of our lives will we gain the strength and unity needed to solve many of the existing problems. It was the Church to which our forefathers turned; it was the Church and their faith down through history which was, at times, their only hope.

It is with this in mind and through faith that we must come together in unity, with faith in the leaders God has chosen to help us bring about the freedom of all men, knowing that we are not and will not be, the slaves of men but only of God whom we serve.

> For by grace have you been saved through faith; and this is not your own doing; it is the gift of God—not because of works, lest any man should boast. For we are his workmanship, created in Christ Jesus for good works, which God prepared beforehand, that we should walk in them. *Eph. 2:8–10*

I am thankful for my ordination to the priesthood, and I am personally thankful that God has allowed me to serve Him and His people during these difficult and frightening times of unrest. I bid your prayers for God's direction and guidance to me in leading you. "I exhort therefore, that, first of all, supplications, prayers, intercession, and giving of thanks be made for all men...."

No matter what, let us never forget to give thanks to God because, indeed, there is always so much to be thankful for. We thank Him for sustaining us, for strengthening us when we grow weak and discouraged, and for giving us faith to face the tasks which are before us.

It is said that looking back keeps us from looking ahead, but I don't really think we can look ahead unless we do look back. A glimpse into our past reminds us of the important years from the early nineteen hundreds until now: the faith, prayers and much justifiable work those years represent. We must look back to the foundation laid for us, the road paved with so much pain and humiliation, and the enduring faith of our fathers which lifted them up in their darkest hours and kept them going in the face of impossible odds.

I say we should look back for example and inspiration, not in complacency and in the belief that nothing has to change. Realizing that we do not live in the same sort of world as the world of our founding fathers, we know we are facing different needs. Hence there is, after looking back, a continuing need to look to the present and to the future. We are witnessing rapid changes of thought, communication, transportation, and daily living. The role of the Church ought to be that of being alert to the significance of each change; of reaching out each year to greet its own generation, eager to understand and deal with the doubts, yearnings, and aspirations of each new generation. Unfortunately and all too often, I do not see the Church doing this. This little jingle I came across says it for me:

> Our fathers have been Churchmen
> Nineteen hundred years or so,
> And to every new proposal
> They have always answered, "*no!*"

That is *not* our reason for looking back. As Christians, we always have to be alert to the signs of the times, and to show the application of the Gospel to the needs of each new day. It is in Christian confidence, therefore, and not in pagan fear that the Church member accepts social change of his own day and, yes, we have reason for looking back, but it is the needs and problems of today that we must be concerned with.

Each member in a parish should strive to be as Joshua when he faced an unexpected responsibility, since each member is an instrument to carry out the functions of God and His Church. If we truly believe that no man was created to be slave to other men we must accept the responsibility of coming together and working together in unity to be free.

I have tried to meet the needs of our parish, which are many and varied, as well as some of the crying needs of our brothers and sisters in the community surrounding our parish. Equally important, I have tried to apply my ministry to the racism of our times that continues to keep blacks not only from progressing, but also compels them to slip backward in the areas of education, housing and employment. I have attempted to involve our entire parish family in the lives of each other and also in the lives of the community outside our walls.

Like Joshua, you were faced with an unexpected responsibility when the Poor People's March was made to Washington. The churches were asked to assist, and you of the parish family worked with some fifty volunteers long hours over hot stoves preparing food. You donated bedding, clothing, and you opened up your church to feed and sleep roughly 250 people, even placing cots in the nave when we ran out of other space. Some of you ladies who had not been in the kitchen for many years left your homes in the wee hours the next morning to prepare breakfast before they left. I thank God for your willingness to join in this community effort, giving of yourselves so generously. The atmosphere was so warm that being a part of the sharing gave a feeling of interpersonal involvement which was beautiful and moving experience. This was the first time many of the people working with us had been inside Holy Cross, and I know from their remarks to me how warmly you welcomed them and worked with them.

F.A.T., Forever Action Together, the merger of many black community organizations, was born here in the Holy Cross under-croft. I know how painful it was for some of you to accept having "your church" used for such meetings, especially when I told you that if the walls downstairs could talk, they would echo much of the anger, bitterness, frustrations and despair expressed there—not always in the prettiest language. And I told you we would not admit the white press, because we did not want to be misquoted and misunderstood. But with God's Grace and your forbearance, out of these stormy meetings has emerged a working group, stronger than ever, still trying to unify the black communities to action for their common improvement. There are several members of Holy Cross serving on committees of F.A.T., and I am grateful for your commitment in accepting this responsibility.

Words do not come easily to express how proud I am of our Young Adult Group. This group (some members and some nonmembers of the parish) organized and met here in our undercroft with dinner, discussion and socializing. When it came to the group's attention that a sponsor was being sought for houses in the immediate neighbor-hood of our parish which were to be rehabilitated, you agreed to undertake this task. These Martin Luther King, Jr., homes were vital in upgrading the living conditions in our community, and you gave much of yourselves to this project. We had no real expertise in this field and the many pitfalls might have discouraged others. Many lessons were learned in such a venture—the hard way! These young people were probing, alert, and determined and did not yield to attempted intimidation and not-so-subtle threats thrown at them by the power bloc. They stood their ground when they discovered they were not being dealt with honestly and refused to be a part of deceiving the very people they had set out to help. They were so persistent, indeed, that they succeeded in having the federal govern-ment intervene and force compliance with rules and regulations. Maybe even more than Joshua they were faced with *unexpected* responsibility, but thanks be to God and His guidance, they accepted the responsibility and met the challenge.

By this time, I pray that our parish family understands my ministry, which cannot be limited to within these walls because so much of what happens outside is part of our Christian responsibility and has a direct effect on our lives. The commission to me as priest and to you as lay ministers is to direct a share of time and service and treasury to those less able than we to help. This is borne out in Paul's Epistle to the Romans: "We then that are strong ought to bear the infirmities of the weak, and not to please ourselves. Let every one of us please his neighbor for *his* good to edification. For even Christ pleased not himself. . . . "

I remind you again and again, as I remind myself, that any good we may have done is not of our own doing—"lest any man should boast"—it is of God's doing. Reverting to Paul's message to the Ephesians, "we are . . . created in Christ Jesus for good works, which God prepared beforehand. . . . "

Congregations are made up of many people with different feelings and experiences. Some of the people are receptive to new ideas and to change; some are not. Some of the people disagree with what is being done, and they say so openly and honestly, asking questions and offering suggestions, because their intent is good and they have the Church's well-being in mind. Others disagree for disagreement's sake, not openly and offering nothing but criticism. It can only be assumed that such persons do *not* have the Church's well-being in mind.

We are called to unity by God as set forth in Scripture: "Now I beseech you, brethren, by the name of our Lord Jesus Christ, that ye all speak the same thing, and there be no divisions among you: but that ye be perfectly joined together in the same mind and in the same judgment." "Is Christ divided?" (Corinthians) And in Romans we find: "Now the God of patience and consolation grant you to be like-minded one toward another according to Christ Jesus: that ye may with one mouth glorify God, even the Father of our Lord Jesus Christ. Wherefore receive ye one another, as Christ also received us to the glory of God."

As your servant in the Lord's service, I have read the Word of God, tried to hear what that Word is saying to me and then put It into proper action. There are many different opinions as to what that "Word" means and says, but one thing I have learned is that anger, unkindness, lack of charity and disunity only lead to more of the same.

If we are to change man's inhumanity to man and attain the freedom so long sought, we have no other choice than to heed God's call to unity, God's call to minister to our neighbor, and God's call to *love*. We have no other choice than to lay aside the small differences which divide us in the face of the enormous task which lies ahead.

I would ask of you, the parish family of the Church of the Holy Cross, that you look back with gratitude to our forefathers and look forward with hope and the love of God in your hearts, "forbearing one another, and forgiving one another if any man have a quarrel against any; even as Christ forgave you, so also do ye. And above all these things, put on charity, which is the bond of perfectness" (Col. 3:13–14).

I charge you one and all and I charge the community of Homewood-Brushton as I charge myself, to *hear God's Word* and *do his will,* with Him as our Foundation, our Rock, and our loving Shepherd. With the peace of God, and charity in our hearts, we will move forward in Christian unity.

> Grace be unto you, and peace, from God our Father,
> and from the Lord Jesus Christ. I thank my God
> always on your behalf, for the grace of God which
> is given you by Jesus Christ.

16

FRANKLIN D. TURNER

Franklin Turner, staff officer for black ministries at the Episcopal Church Center in New York, was born in North Carolina in 1933. He was graduated from Livingstone College and the Berkeley Divinity School. He has done graduate studies at West Virginia University and the General Theological Seminary. He has held pastorates in Texas and Washington, D.C. In 1972, he came to New York to serve at the Executive Council of the Church, and in 1974, assumed his present position. He has been in contact with every phase of the Church's work among blacks and is doing an outstanding job in promoting skills among the clergy, recruiting candidates for the ministry, serving as an advisor for the placing of clergy and in organizing seminars and conferences to study the effectiveness of the Church's mission in this area of its work.

This sermon was delivered during a conference on preaching in the black Episcopal tradition held at the College of Preachers in Washington, D.C. It clearly illustrates some of the problems faced by black clergy in bearing witness to the Gospel in terms that have meaning to black constituents.

Let My People Go

Afterward Moses and Aaron went to Pharaoh and said,... "Let my people go, that they may hold a feast unto me in the wilderness."
(Ex. 5:1)

We have been here this week examining and evaluating black preaching in the Episcopal tradition, past and present, and with some discussion about what the future should hold. We have no doubt discovered that many of our Episcopal forefathers were dynamic and committed preachers of God's Word. And many of our contemporaries are too, and this gives us reason to hope for the future.

Underlying our being here and focusing on the enterprise of preaching leads me to think we Episcopal priests have not been as dynamic, inspirational, and convincing preachers as we could be. Preaching is a much-enjoyed, valued, and venerated activity in the black church tradition which we have sorely neglected. It is therefore the feeling of many, including the commission for black ministries, that we must recover and develop this great art and tradition of the black church, and give preaching an honored place in the liturgy and worship of our church.

I will not however dwell on the subject and content of preaching in my remarks—that has already been done throughout this conference—but instead focus my thoughts on the preacher himself.

I have a feeling that every black preacher thinks of himself as a Moses to his people, especially if he has been called by God. A majority of black Americans have always looked upon the preacher as a Moses and themselves as Hebrew slaves in need of being led out of Egypt. A black priest may, however, think of himself as being called by someone else, namely his rector or bishop or friend, which may lead him to think of himself quite differently. He may think of himself as one to be served instead of one who serves; or as rector—one who rules; or as God's gift to the world for whom others must fall down and pay tribute; or even more extreme, as a messiah to whom worship is directed, rather than one to be sacrificed for others. How one thinks of himself will definitely influence his preaching and ministry.

A popular song from the not-too-distant past said that "what the world needs now is love sweet love, that's the only thing that there's not enough of." I would emphatically agree; but quickly say that what the world does not need, and particularly in the black community, is more princes or pimps or would-be messiahs, but more leaders and preachers like Moses, Malcolm and Martin and Kenneth Hughes— strong committed leaders and preachers who can hear the cries of their people, see and respond to their afflictions, and boldly proclaim the message, "Thus saith the Lord God of Israel, Let my people go, that they may hold a feast unto me in the wilderness."

We all know that you can't hold a feast in the oppressor's presence or on his property. You can't really get down and sing the songs of Zion in a strange land. Only in the wilderness, the passage toward freedom, can we really have a feast and celebration. Only free individuals and people have something to celebrate and can make a feast to the Lord—not slaves.

God wants us to celebrate and he created us to make a feast to Him by sending us the Prince of Peace. He has given us His greatest gift— His Son Jesus Christ. He has provided us with the Messiah who made the supreme sacrifice. He conquered sin, death, the grave and all other forces which would enslave us individually and collectively as a people. God has and is liberating us and his people. This is the unadulterated message we must live and proclaim as black preachers, no matter what the cost or sacrifice to us personally.

The black preacher who thinks of himself as a Moses to his people—and I believe we all should—must be sensitive to the cries of his people; he must be clear about his own identity and role as a leader, and must be called and committed to carrying on God's liberating work among his people and in the world. He must be prepared and willing to confront the Pharaohs of the day, wherever and whoever they may be, and say, "Let my people go!" Assuredly, this is an overwhelming and frightening task. But take heart, my brothers, for the God who called you will go with you, send a companion with you, speak for you if needs be, sustain you, and prop you up on every leaning side.

I should tell you that Moses couldn't go and speak to Pharaoh until he discovered his own identity, saw the needs of his people, accepted God's plan for him and them. God had a need and plan for him, and for us as well.

I can imagine what terrible shock and revelation it must have been for Moses to discover that he was Hebrew instead of Egyptian. He must have been shaken to the very foundation of his being, even if he were nursed and nurtured by his own mother, and had some clues about his Hebrew roots. To have been raised as a prince and brought up in a palace and in manhood find out that you are one of the least of these my brothers, is devastating to the human spirit.

I remember as a child my mother dragging me from the front to the back of the bus, and explaining to me why I couldn't sit behind the driver—that I was colored. You know the story and the feeling. Nearly every little boy wants to sit behind the driver whether it's the bus driver or the engineer on a train. He wants to imagine what it's like to be in control of this powerful machine. Control and power is the name of the game. Control and power over one's life and destiny. Ever since that incident I have been coming to grips with my own identity. And I believe that that incident on the bus helped me to begin to discover who I am, and greatly influenced my choice of vocation—the ministry.

Moses came to grips with his identify not in the palace, but in the market place of life where he saw one of his fellow Hebrews being beaten unmercifully. It was at that moment he realized and found his identity, and struck a blow for it.

There is a story told of an eagle's egg which got mixed up with some chicken's eggs, and eventually they all hatched. From the time they were hatched there was something different about the eagle, but he did not know it and therefore grew up acting like a chicken. One day an eagle flew overhead and made the sounds and noises that only eagles can make. Something strange began stirring in this eagle on the ground, but as the eagle passed over, the one on the ground went back to scratching the ground and acting like a chicken. Several times eagles flew over and this young eagle had these strange feelings within—but continued scratching the ground for food. But one day as an eagle flew over and the stirrings were so great in this young eagle that he began flopping his wings—wings that he didn't know he had—and rose up and soared up, and joined the other eagle. He must have felt like Alex Haley did when he discovered his family in Gambia—

and exclaimed—"Thank God I have found you—Kunta Kinte. Thank God I have found my family. Now I know who I am, because I know who my family is."

God did not create us to be less than human—scratching around in the dirt of dehumanization, but to soar and live on the highest level of life—like the eagle.

I have observed in the last ten years or so, black priests who attempted to be anything except black: mulatto, Negro, colored, and it usually took an unpleasant incident in their life in this church to make them come to grips with their blackness. Let's face it—black Episcopalians live in Pharaoh's house, and it doesn't matter whether you were born in it or elected to come into it, as I did. And often it takes an unpleasant incident to bring home to us that we are not Anglican, but black. For most of us this is a bitter pill to swallow. We keep hoping it will come back up rather than go down. The remote possibility of being adopted by Pharaoh's daughter or marrying her, makes it even more difficult to swallow this black pill. My advice to you is to swallow it quickly; don't prolong the agony, so that you can get on with self-identity and the work of liberation for our people, remembering that only a Hebrew can lead the Hebrews out of Egypt and not an Egyptian.

Like Moses, many of us black Episcopalians have the double advantage of knowing our people as well as the Egyptians. Some of us have been fortunate enough to get the best education the court and palace can provide. Adopted by the Princess and educated in the palace, we are not to forget our own people and their great burden. Black priests and people ought to use their double advantage for the building of a people, and not for their own personal gains.

I can assure you that the attraction and lure of being adopted by the Episcopal Church is exceedingly great, especially if she waves the purple or red in front of you, offers you a seat on the council or on the cabinet.

Don't misunderstand me, I am not saying to refuse these offers, unless you suspect you are being bought or co-opted because by law and righteousness they belong to you. But there is a difference between being co-opted and adopted. I caution you to remember who you are, especially when and while you are in those positions and offices.

Moreover, after discovering his real identity, Moses could no longer sit in high places and disinterestedly watch his fellow man being abused and misused. He had to do something about it, even if it was while the establishment was not looking. He had to leave the country. If one really identifies with his people and does something meaningful to change their condition and status in this racist society, he may well have to leave town or the country, whatever that may represent today. Take, for example, all the black men and women who fill our jails and prisons, or who have been killed because they attempted to improve the lot of black people. Malcolm, Martin, and Ben Chavis, to name but three.

While in exile, Moses perfected his identity, was called by God, went to seminary and studied under the tutelage of Jethro the Midianite priest, was ordained and commissioned by God and sent back to Egypt. He went back reluctantly with his companion Aaron, but singing with assurance and faith, "I know the Lord has laid his hands on me."

It is not easy for one to go back to his homeland, to his friends and enemies, and act and say something differently. Everyone remembers who you were and what you were. The people asked of Jesus, "Is not this Jesus, the son of Joseph, the carpenter?" when He attempted to lay some heavy teaching on them.

Of course, Moses was very conscious of the situation of a prophet being without honor in his own country. Therefore he asked Jahweh, "What shall I tell the people and Pharaoh when they ask who sent me?" The response was, "Tell them that I AM hath sent you."

Moses' most difficult problem was not getting Pharaoh to let the people go, because God was taking care of that. Rather, it was getting the Hebrews to let go of their slave mentality, and work for their own freedom. They wanted freedom without having to leave Egypt and go through the wilderness to the Promised Land. This is the most difficult task for black Episcopal priests, getting their people out of the mental state of "it would have been better if we had stayed in Egypt."

This is why it is so necessary for the preacher-priest to be sure of his identity and calling so as to keep the faint-hearted and weak on the right path and right task.

Moses never got to see his ragged group become a solid nation, and neither did he reach the Promised Land with them. Eventually they did get to the Promised Land, and they became a great nation. Many of us may not get to the Promised Land of personhood and nationhood with our people, but, be assured, they will get there.

Martin Luther King, Jr., said in his last sermon, in his last struggle for the dignity and fair treatment of black garbage workers, that he may not make it to the Promised Land with them, but they would get there. We have not yet made it but we are farther along in the wilderness because of his leadership and preaching.

I challenge us as black preachers and priests to be certain of our own identity, clear about who called us, and convincing in proclaiming the message we have been given—let my people go!

17

ROBERT C. CHAPMAN

Robert C. Chapman was born and reared in Brooklyn, New York. He is a graduate of Brooklyn College and General Theological Seminary. He holds a master's degree in sociology from Brooklyn College, and has done extensive graduate work at the University of Pennsylvania and New York University in the fields of American history and American literature. He has had many articles published in various denominational magazines, and has held adjunct professorships at both Fordham and New York universities. He has been a parish priest in Hempstead, New York, and in the inner cities of Detroit and New York. He has also been a chaplain at the University of Pennsylvania and an executive of the National Council of Churches. He is now the archdeacon of Manhattan, supervising the mission strategy of the church's work in the largest urban area in the country.

This sermon, delivered before the annual meeting of the Union of Black Episcopalians in Rochester, New York, in 1977, illustrates the dynamics of the age that arose out of the new sense of black awareness.

We Are the Branches

Among the most descriptive, and perhaps prophetic words ever written about the black American have come to us from the poetic hand of James Weldon Johnson. Appropriately enough, they are also prayerful words, and we know them well:

> God of our weary years,
> God of our silent tears;
> Thou who hast brought us, thus far,
>   on the way . . .
> Sheltered beneath thy hand,
> May we forever stand
> True to our God,
> True to our native land.

The words are descriptive because we are a people who have always called upon God. God has been our strength, on the right hand and on the left. He has been our "very present help in trouble" (Ps. 46:1)— and we have never failed to "Go, tell it on the mountain!"

We have not forgotten our origins. Our spiritual roots are in God. We are assembled here in Rochester because, in part, and in the first instance, we are a spiritual family. As part of the spiritual family of God, we are associated with who God is, and what God does. No confusion in our minds about that all—not since our Jesus clarified it all by telling us, straight out: "I am the vine, ye are the branches: . . . without me ye can do nothing" (Jn. 15:5).

Yes, Lord, spiritually we know who we are : "We are the branches."—Ain't no "branches" if there ain't no vine. Ain't no "branches" if there ain't no trunk.—Ain't no *us* if there ain't no *God!*—And we are here, so, just like ole Job, "[We] know that our redeemer lives!"

But it's been hard in this place—it's been hard. That's what Johnson meant when he wrote about our "weary years."

And it's been painful in this place. Oh! How it has hurt, just plain hurt, sometimes! And we have tried, in the power of God, to be strong. We have tried, in the strength of our God, not to cry out either in pain or in anger all of the time. But sometimes, as children, we have come bouncing into the kitchen, joyously calling to that beautiful, black woman, whose name is "Mama," only to come to a jolting and shocked halt, as we see her desperately trying to hide from our puzzled and quick eyes, the water that is there, in her own soft eyes. It was because Papa lost his job again; or because "B.J." cuts classes all the time now and just "hangs out." Or it was because Cousin Ellen died in the waiting room of the City Hospital after sitting there for two hours without attention following what proved to be a heart attack.—And mere children that we were, we walked slowly and sadly out of the kitchen—so hurt, so hurt—as the water now grew heavy in our own eyes.

Johnson described it; "God of our silent tears," James Weldon Johnson described it!

And yet, isn't it true? It is God, only the power of God Almighty, that "hast brought us thus far on the way!" "We are the branches," and it has been the vibrant strength of his indwelling spirit, like the rich sap, coursing through the vine, nourishing the otherwise dying branches, that has kept us from drying up, falling apart and disintegrating altogether.

It has been hard and painful in the past; the sun has not shone in all of its fulness today; and we don't know, yet, what tomorrow will bring—but one thing we do know; we know our spiritual roots. We know that "We are the branches"—and we vow, along with St. Paul, who first said it, that:

> Neither death, nor life, nor angels, nor principalities, nor powers, nor things present, nor things to come, nor height, nor depth, nor any other creature shall be able to separate us from the love of God, which is in Christ Jesus our Lord. (Rom. 8:38–39)

And, praise God, as it has been written, so it shall be done, in us; and the angels themselves will have to say, "Amen!"

But there comes next, in this verse by Johnson, a description of us which is also a bit prophetic: We want to be "True to our God—True to our native land." This is an accurate description of us. We have always tried to be "True to our God"—and we have always tried to be true to this "native land," whether we were born here, in fact, or immigrated here by choice.

We have tried to keep the two loyalties equal in strength and co-balanced since our sojourn here began. Look at the flags behind me! We have tried to be "True to our God," and "True to our native land," even when this "native land" has behaved toward us as though there is no God! And that effort has caused great tensions among us, sometimes, driving some of us away from others of us at times. Worse yet, driving some of us, as individuals, to the point where the forces of our own minds are waging tumultuous inner war with the forces of our own hearts—while our souls, shaken to the depth with every volley, clutch desperately to hold fast to truth, to weather the storm, and to keep us close to Jesus!

At times like that, we know well what Langston Hughes meant when he had a strong black mother say to her unsettled son:

> ... Boy, don't you turn back.
> Don't you set down on the steps
> 'cause you finds it kinder hard.
> Don't you fall now—
> For I'se still climbin',
> And life for me ain't been no crystal stair.
> ("Mother to Son")

It is a dilemma we have had to live with for as long as we have been in America. And it is a dilemma we are going to face as long as there is an America—because we ain't going nowhere. And, no matter what the odds continue to be, while we are here, we intend to get somewhere.

Within the last year we have had graphic and dramatic cause to see and to sense, with new insight, that, although this is, indeed, our "native land," it has never been our "mother land." We were the only boll weevil in the cotton patch who didn't have a home! All the other weevils used to look at us and say:

> I'm German-American; I'm Anglo-American;
> I'm Franco-American; I'm Italo-American—
> I know my national roots. But you—
> What's your ancestry, boy?
> What are your roots?

Then, last fall, Brother Alex fixed all that. His book began with these simple but spine-tingling words:

> Early in the spring of 1750, in the village of Juffure, four days upriver from the coast of the Gambia, West Africa, a manchild was born to Omoro and Binta Kinte...and there was the prideful knowledge that the name of Kinte would thus be distinguished and perpetuated.

Oh, they have changed the "Kinte" into "Haley," or "Smith," or "Richardson," or "Chapman," or "Greene," or "Weston"—and a hundred-thousand, and more other names—but it doesn't matter any more. We've found it for sure, now. We, too, know our *roots*.

"We are the branches." Spiritually, we are the branches of the empowering vine of Salvation, which is Jesus, the Christ.

Historically, we are the branches of the strong enduring trees that had their origins in the rich, fertile soils of that vast continent in which, archaeologists tell us, human life, itself, began—the land of Omoro; the land of Binta; the land of Kunta Kinte!

That makes us an African people—it makes us black. They have always accepted this fact—although some of us have tried to run, and to hide from it. But "they" have always known it. And they have always related to us on the basis of their acceptance of the fact that we are black—because some of us have always been—and still are—trying to hide from it (especially when around them, where our affected speech and mannerisms are not subject to the view of the rest of us)—because of this, our struggle has often been more grueling than it ought to have been; now, a gazelle has a better chance of survival when he does not walk nonchalantly among a pride of lions hoping to be mistaken for a lion.

When you get right down to it, survival is what it is still really all about for us in this land. When they cleared the forests to make the great cities of this country; when they cleared the forests to create the great farmlands of the South and the Midwest; and to make the railroads, the intricate networks of superhighways, and the airports— when they did these things to build the nation that is now our "native land," what do you think happened to the trees, vines and bushes that were in the way? They were knocked down and used up. Well, "We are the branches," and, as Ronald Fair has written, we are "many thousand gone."

We are "many thousand gone," and going, into public school systems in cities all over this "native land" of ours, where the phrase "quality education" is more and more a cruel euphemism meaning "pay teachers and administrators more, and teach those unruly and dumb kids less." And our survival in a technocracy, that demands increasingly more knowledge, increasingly more technical, business, and language skills, is solidly on the line. The broken-down, inept public school systems of the cities of this country are now where the majority of our young, sapling branches are. By and large, the majority of student populations of the decrepit public school systems in the cities of America are black and Hispanic. While the instructional and administrative staffs remain predominantly, if not increasingly, white.

We are "many thousand gone," and going, to the violations-ridden, landlord-forsaken apartment houses and tenements of the inner cities, whence businesses flee, prices go ever higher, and any public transportation worth its name, is a dream of long ago, before the whites went.

We are "many thousand gone," and going, to the dogs, cats, and rats that rummage through the filth and garbage in the vacant, crumbling bricks-filled lots, that in some cases, can be counted in block after broken inner-city block.

Our children, our young sapling branches, are "many thousand gone," and going, withering and drying-up under the conscienceless onslaughts of the pushers, the well-to-do suppliers, and the politicians and officials of every level who engage in or wink at the drugs traffic which can only be called a form of chemical warfare against our children.

These crimes are perpetrated not only against blacks and Hispanics. To be sure, numerically, there are many poor whites sucked up and whisked away in the process. Bu we have to take our heads out of the sand, and stop thinking of sheer numbers. We have to check out the meaning of proportions in order to know what is happening to us.

In recent years, in the face of massive para-military power such as was used in Detroit, Jackson State College, and other places; and in the face of a few conciliatory bones that were thrown to a piddling few of the better educated of us and to a few of the more vocally militant, if not actually more militant among us, as well as because a few helpful laws were passed, we backed away from the vigorous pursuit of our full civil rights—and now, business has begun to go on, "as usual."

"As usual," in the economically devastating times we face, black unemployment has continued to be double that of whites. Yet, with the unemployment rate for blacks double that of white females, the women's rights movement of today is more popular, and is reaping more benefits for its advocates than is the civil rights movement of blacks. Had I a vote as a deputy to the last General Convention, I would have voted a sure "yes" on the ordination of women. I know of no theological or moral reason for voting "no." But the certain fact is that there are more women entering our seminaries and institutes of theology. A fact of equal stature is that they are not black. A final, dismal fact is that there are fewer and fewer blacks, counting males and females, who are preparing for Holy Orders. Our branches are withering right on the vine.

"We are the branches," and branches are called upon to blossom, bear fruit, and multiply. As branches, we are under the all-seeing eye of the Husbandman, the Husbandman who has said: "By their fruits ye shall know them"; the Husbandman who, "when he saw a fig tree in the way...and found nothing thereon, but leaves only,...said unto it, Let no fruit grow on thee henceforward for ever. And presently the fig tree withered away" (Mt. 21:19).

Pretence! Sham! Not being what we are called upon to be—that's what raises the hackles of our God.

If the branches, themselves, do not go about the business of bearing fruit, those branches are good for nothing but to be chopped down, cut up, and put into the fire. That is to say: If we, ourselves, do not get on with the business of nurturing the minds of our children; if we do not enter into or get behind the public school systems and make them produce education for our children; if we do not enter into or get behind those aspects of the criminal justice system which make it a system that has declared an open season for slamming bars behind blacks; if we do not force through programs that will rehabilitate and build the housing in our rotting inner cities—where they keep the masses of black people; if we do not enter into the ministry of our Lord—the social ministry as well as the sacerdotal ministry—if we do not rise to do these things, we are as branches that bare no fruit. And another way of saying we will be "put into the fire" is to say we will undoubtely go to hell!

We need not tell ourselves how hard a task it is, how hostile and unfertile is the opportunity offered by the social soil around us—the determined tree will spread its outreaching branches from the craggy rocks of the mountain's shady slope! "We are the branches," and we are called upon by God, himself, to accept primary responsibility for the nurture of the fruit that springs from our limbs.

We need not tell ourselves that the social dangers are too great: the danger of being misunderstood; the danger of being misinterpreted; the danger of distasteful confrontation, when what we want is peace! Peace at what price? I don't know who wrote it; I saw it on a poster that showed a turtle walking; and what is said is wisdom and good advice for us: "Behold the turtle! He never makes progress unless he sticks his neck out!" We have come this far "sheltered beneath his hand." "We have come this far by faith." Reflecting on our past, there is reason for fear. Reflecting on our past, there is reason for faith. What it boils down to, then, is which has the greater power over us— fear or faith?

St. Paul addressed himself to that question, and he told us what it's all about: "For ye have not received the spirit of bondage again to fear; But ye have received the spirit of adoption, whereby we cry, 'Abba,' 'Father.'"

There is an old Japanese proverb, whose origins are anonymous, that I would like to leave in the minds of any of us who may yet be anxious or timorous in the face of the knowledge of the foreboding, yet necessary, task that stands towering over us: "Fear knocked at the door. Faith answered and found no one there."

My brothers, my sisters, in the power of our God, we have much work to do—this week and from then on in. Amen!

18

WALTER D. DENNIS

Walter D. Dennis is a native of Washington, D.C., where he was born in 1932. He is a graduate of Virginia State College, and holds an M.A. degree in North American history and constitutional law from New York University. He is a graduate of the General Theological Seminary and a candidate for the Ph.D. degree at New York University. He has received a D.D. degree from the Interdenominational Theological Center in Atlanta. He has had pastorates in Brooklyn, New York City, and Hampton, Virginia, and has held adjunct professorships at Hampton Institute and General Theological Seminary. He has served in many responsible positions in the diocese of New York, the national Episcopal Church, and the National Council of Churches. His wide range of interests is reflected in his memberships on boards of organizations concerned with drugs, abortion, homosexuality, juvenile justice, and racism. While serving as canon residentiary of the Cathedral Church of St. John the Divine he also planned and executed conferences in these fields. He is a member of the Union of Black Episcopalians and the convenor of the black caucus in the diocese of New York. He was consecrated suffragan bishop of New York in 1979.

In this sermon he directs the attention of the congregation to a subject that is not particularly the concern of blacks, except as they are part of American society, but is illustrative of the broad outlook that our clegy is developing in their leadership in the larger community. As canon of the cathedral, and as a suffragan bishop of New York, he is in a position to speak to the whole church—a situation hardly in the fondest dreams of those who struggled against racism in the church 175 years ago.

The Church's Attitude Toward Drugs

And God saw everything that he had made,
and behold, it was very good.
(Gen. 1:31)

A new book has just been published by Doubleday entitled *The Sacred Mushroom and the Cross,* which suggests that drugs played a role in the early history of Christianity. It is hard to tell from reading this book whether it stands in the tradition of Christianity-debunkers like the recently published *Passover Plot,* or if it is in the tradition of Albert Schweitzer's "nineteenth-century" Jesus and S. F. Brandon's "revolutionary" Jesus, which is in both cases a seeing of Christ as "a reflection of the liberal protestant face seen at the bottom of a deep well" [George Tyrell].

This book does raise for us the question of contemporary attitudes toward drug abuse and use. Certainly everyone here is aware that drugs have played a role in the history of religion and literature, drugs such as the sacred *soma* of India and peyote in America. I am told that marijuana is still smoked regularly by priests in temples dedicated to Shiva in India. Thomas De Quincey and Coleridge both wrote about their experiences with drugs.

The pressing question for us is: how should the Church in the 1970s respond? We are all fully aware that more and more young people are puffing marijuana. And it is specifically about *this* drug that I wish to speak this morning.

Now, what is the evidence? In this country alone there are perhaps ten million youngsters, maybe twenty million, who smoke marijuana regularly. The laws are discriminatory, for they allow us to inhale nicotine and swill alcohol but clamp people in jail for marijuana use until recently in North Dakota one could receive 99 years at hard labor for a first offense with marijuana!

Most of the laws fail to discriminate between nonaddictive and addictive, between mind and body drugs, and the laws are unevenly enforced. Middle-class adults who smoke pot, or grass, as it is sometimes called, get away with it. Teenagers are often caught and in some instances receive sentences of up to five years in prison, ruining their lives. Our laws are obviously panicky and irrational in this area.

For these reasons I believe that, until there is compelling medical evidence that marijuana is harmful, the use of it should not be illegal. But marijuana *abuse* should. By this, I mean that laws governing marijuana abuse should be essentially the same as those governing the abuse of alcohol.

Furthermore, I believe that all those who are currently serving long sentences because of felony convictions for use of marijuana before enlightened laws were passed should be given amnesty, or at the least, should have their sentences drastically reduced.

I realize that the General Convention of our Church which will be meeting in Houston for the next two weeks has a full agenda, but I do hope that some attention will be given to this subject of pressing for more equitable and realistic laws, and for amnesty in the cases of undue punishment, for this is of deep concern to so many of our young people.

Some of you are perhaps aware that the U.S. government is testing all kinds of marijuana from different parts of the world to find its common elements. One of the benefits of my proposal for legislation is that the government could then supervise the quality of marijuana smoked without in any way sanctioning the action of smoking. We have ample precedent of this kind in the supervision of 100 proof liquors. Also, I might suggest that the advertising and promotion of marijuana be prohibited, and that packages carry the warning: Caution! Marijuana may be harmful to your health.

One may ask, why legalize? if the U.S. government is still studying the effects. The reply is that the studies are so late in coming! As a matter of fact, what brought about the studies is not that marijuana seemed harmful, but the surprising fact that it did not appear harmful, which so upset society's preconceived notions that it finally decided to find some proof.

It is ironic that our present anti-marijuana laws are upheld chiefly by the older generation, and flouted and condemned by the young, for it is the older generation which should understand the issue most clearly, having lived through the era of alcohol prohibition. They saw with their own eyes that the entire nation—not just the drinkers and sellers of liquor—suffered moral and mental harm from that particular outbreak of rampant puritanism. They should remember that attempts to legislate morality resulted only in widespread disrespect for the law, new markets and new profits for gangsters, and wholesale bribery and corruption, so that the government became a greater object of contempt than criminals.

The marijuana laws, much like those of prohibition, are unpopular and therefore ignored. Many law enforcement officers don't want them. Many responsible parents oppose them, and a great number of young people feel that they are not worth paying any attention to. And as we should well know, an unenforceable law breeds a very dangerous contempt for the majesty of the law.

A final question which is certain to be raised is: What about juveniles and their right to use and possess marijuana? I believe that whatever is the legal drinking age within a state should be the age at which one can also legally smoke marijuana if one wishes.

In making this radical proposal I realize that there are dangers. The same type of personality who may abuse alcohol after one drink may, after trying marijuana, want to take a really dangerous drug. This is a risk we must accept.

The old adage that "the hard case makes bad law" applies here. Also, we must remember that the law and government can never take the place of the responsibility each of us ultimately bears for our own lives.

In closing, let me say that I am not advocating that we replace the traditional coffee hour after church services with a turned-on smoke-in, but I *am* saying that if an adult comes to the coffee hour and decides to smoke marijuana instead of cigarettes, he/she should not be subject to criminal liability.

Is this too much to ask for in a society where people depend on moments of emotional release from a very tense way of life? It would be preferable to find ways toward fantasy and rapture which do not rely on chemicals and external stimulants, just as it would be nice to induce gaiety and relaxation without martinis and bourbon, but that would require a very different society from the one we have today.

Therefore, it seems very hypocritical for a whole population which uses pep pills, tranquilizers, and alcohol to impose such vengeance on a group which prefers another stimulant which may be indeed less harmful than the commonly accepted ones.

Perhaps the task for Christians and churchpeople is not to condemn marijuana use but rather to find what, if any, is the *good* use of marijuana. Then we might know the meaning of the text, "And God saw everything that he had made, and behold, it was very good."

19

HAROLD LOUIS WRIGHT

Harold L. Wright was born in Boston in 1929, and was educated in the local schools of that city. He attended the New England Conservatory of Music, and received the A.B. degree from Boston University. He was a graduate of the General Theological School and received the S.T.D. from that institution. His ministry was contained in the diocese of Long Island where he assumed many responsibilities beyond his parish work. He was a member of the Standing Committee and the Board of Examining Chaplains. He was consecrated suffragan bishop of the diocese of New York in 1974. Bishop Wright died in 1979.

This sermon was delivered before the convention of the diocese of New York in 1976. Its simple recall to basic spirituality is the magnet that draws every element of the church's tasks into a unity of purpose. Black and white can understand their fellowship in the Gospel though different strategies may be employed, so long as the common goal is constantly set before them. This is the strong, positive character of a church that continues to contain different races, ethnic groups, and social classes within its borders.

The Test of Evangelism

Brothers and sisters in Christ Jesus, power to you and blessings on you from God our father and from the Lord Jesus Christ.

There is a sign on Route 212 in Ulster County which advertises the location and hours of service of a church in Saugerties. In large red letters on a white background the sign proclaims, "We preach Christ, Crucified, Risen and Coming Again." I have driven past that sign countless times over the last decade, but I have never seen the church which it advertises. I have never been moved to want to seek out that church because the sign is weatherbeaten and bears all the marks of neglect. The lettering, once bright red, is now all faded, the wood is splitting and the paint chipped and peeling. I have wondered many times whether the preaching of the Gospel in that church is in the same condition as the sign and, by extension, I have been led to muse on the proclamation of the Gospel in congregations in the diocese of New York.

"We preach Christ, Crucified, Risen and Coming Again."

Matthew tells us that when John's disciples asked Jesus to show them his identification papers, that they might know if he was the one whom they sought, Jesus told them, "the blind receive their sight, and the lame walk, the lepers are cleansed, and the deaf hear, the dead are raised up, and the poor have the gospel preached to them."

In the Episcopal Church we have a great love of highly organized campaigns, expensively funded, decked out with catchy slogans. We enter into them enthusiastically, with expectations of early if not instantly measurable success. Recall just a few of the recent ones— Parish Life Conferences; Mutual Responsibility and Interdependence in the Body of Christ (M.R.I.); Partners in Mission; Companion Dioceses; General Convention Special Program; Mission, Service and Strategy—to say nothing of the Church's Teaching Series and the Seabury Series.

But we have a short attention span, and we use an inadequate measuring rod when we evaluate our efforts; and so programs come and programs go, slogans come and slogans go because they have not produced the instantly expected success in terms of new people or more money. While we pursued those campaigns and touted those slogans, how much effort was spent in seeing that the blind received their sight, and the lame walked, the lepers were cleansed, the deaf made to hear, the dead raised up and the poor had the gospel preached to them?

When we tire of the programs and the slogans, we create and concentrate on issues. Today, most of the energy and much of the finances of this church are dedicated to whether we shall have a new prayer book and whether women shall be ordained to the priesthood and to the episcopate. I do not seek to minimize in any way the importance of either of these matters, but I am constrained to say that, in my judgment, they are not the major issues facing the church today, and I wonder to what extent our vigorous pursuit of them is a way of avoiding coming to grips with other issues more vitally affecting the people for whom God's Christ died, and rose and promised to come again! And as at the national level in our church life we have turned to a kind of navel-gazing to avoid grappling with hard and unpopular questions, so even a cursory glance through the resolutions in the calendar of business of this diocesan convention will reveal a heavy concentration on matters of internal machinery with relatively little attention given to those issues which constrict and cripple so many of God's people in their daily lives.

I know that in the church we are not of one mind in what we do or how we do it. I know that we are not agreed on all the implications of the Gospel as it pertains to our times and conditions. Nor do I want to appear to be calling for a simplistic approach to the many problems facing the church today. However, I do remind you that mission is at the heart of the Gospel and the life of the church. A church which is committed to mission is forever bursting beyond its own special interests and concerns. The conscience of a church which is committed to mission is forever alive to social wrongs. The life of a church which is committed to mission is dynamic and vibrant. The measure of what we do is whether, in the broadest sense, "the blind receive their sight, and the lame walk, the lepers are cleansed, and the deaf hear, the dead are raised up, and the poor have the gospel preached to them."

Along many of the roads throughout this great diocese there are signs which advertise the location and the hours of services in local churches. In large letters on a blue and white background they proclaim "The Episcopal Church Welcomes You." I have driven past countless of those signs on innumerable occasions over the years, but until present responsibilities laid the necessity upon me, I was seldom moved to seek out the churches which those signs advertise. Oh, I have been pleased, though sometimes dubious, at the promise of welcome which those signs held out to me. But I have often wondered what was being preached from the pulpits of those churches. Was it the latest craze in political or ethical or social philosophy? Was it the jargon of the muddled thinking of much contemporary theology? Or was it "Christ—Crucified—Risen—and Coming Again"? When people come to our churches from the prisons of their lives and ask to see our identification papers that they might know whether we preach the words of life, shall we be able to tell them that "the blind receive their sight, and the lame walk, the lepers are cleansed, and the deaf hear, the dead are raised up, and the poor have the gospel preached to them"?